Change Our Stories, Change Our World

Change Our Stories, Change Our World

Karen I. Shragg

Freethought House

Minneapolis–St. Paul

Library of Congress Control Number: 2020945550

Cover design by Mary Ellen Gutknecht
Interior design by Robaire Ream

ISBN: 9780988493872

To my parents
Babe and Sarah Shragg
and their amazing story of love

Any large-scale human cooperation–whether a modern state, a medieval church, an ancient city or an archaic tribe—is rooted in common myths that exist only in people's collective imagination.

—Yuval Noah Harari

Table of Contents

Author's Note

The consequences of a mistreated Earth will spare no one. Stories among modern humans, up until now, have accelerated our course of destruction. There is no such thing as forever; time always runs out. The economy cannot grow forever from the plunder of limited resources. The current success of humans, limited as it is to the benefit of a few, will bring about our collective demise.

Our population cannot grow forever. It is already billons over the Earth's carrying capacity. The limits of arable soil, water, open space, and wild places are already tattered and will prevent that, with no help if we place too much faith in green energy. False fixes perpetuate the proliferation of our planetary takeover.

Racism must not continue to perpetuate suffering and cause the death of so many of its innocent victims, and classicism needs to stop defining our world by its most unfair common denominator: money.

Most of all, we cannot remain attached to our old stories of how we live on this planet. We continue to treat this third planet from the sun as if we are an exceptional species. By tossing out Earth's rules, we condemn ourselves to suffering and the ultimate punishment: extinction. Although our extinction would create a renaissance of other life forms innately able to respect ecological boundaries, it seems worthwhile to discuss how we might possibly live within those boundaries.

If we do not challenge our long-held assumptions, we will seal our fate. By any measurements we are doing a lousy job of taking care of our planet and she, in turn, can't do a better job of taking care of us. We say we want change, but we rarely achieve it. We prefer the ineffective known world for the effective unknown world. We choose the convenient over the inconvenient. What we need is a big leap forward beginning with the courage to let go of the following stories if we want to improve our world, and our chances for survival.

Introduction

Everything starts with a story, but even when some are proven wrong, or even evil, they can continue to perpetuate their misery throughout society. This book is an exploration of why that phenomenon has flourished and why it is so important that we learn how to end those destructive narratives that stand in the way of our survival on our ailing homeland, our planet. We need multiple paradigm shifts and they can't happen until we shift our stories.

I define old stories as ones that create misery and suffering for humans and other species. They are unsustainable. Their continued practice over time destroys our ability to share our planet with other species. The definition of unsustainable has become broader over time due to the advancement of weapons, toxic chemicals, and non-biodegradable products. It has further been inflamed by the way the nearly eight billion of us have terra-formed the planet to meet our needs.

The tasks at hand are enormous, overwhelming and terrifying on every level, but the risks for not changing our ways are even greater. We risk rendering this amazing water planet lifeless because the following stories are no longer serving us, which they truly never did. The most powerful photo I have ever seen was a 5,000-year-old dump site of Inuit people in the Northwest Territories. It had only fossilized whale bones and seal carcasses in it. Everything we own today, from our toothpaste tubes to our shoes are made from non-biodegradable materials and were made with carbon releasing fossil fuels. Our landfills could never be as benign as the Inuit's for they pollute and continue to grow along with our numbers.

While I was in the midst of writing this book, a pandemic struck. The surreal effect on daily life has highlighted the weaknesses in the way we live our fragile lives. This experience has reaffirmed my understanding about how severely unsustainable our civilization is; therefore, it is critical that we understand how we got here and how not to repeat our mistakes if the future permits a chance to change our ways.

We have a terrible habit for putting band-aids on our problems and wonder why they never go away.

To examine our stories in depth, we must first move upstream and view humans through the lens of being just one of the many species of planet Earth. A broader view of what we have done collectively since our arrival nearly 200,000 years ago is required. Any other perspective will make many readers bristle at my opinions and suggestions.

My perspective as a life-long naturalist has allowed me the ability to see us for what we are: a very successfully reproductive predatory species able to exploit all biomes and climates. That success, however, is not to be celebrated, for it is the key to our inevitable demise. At the heart of our success is a story of domination combined with an elevated sense of who we are relative to other species.

Cognitive neuroscientist Michael Gazzaniga studies the physiology behind our need to connect to stories. His research concluded that our left brain is set up to interpret our world and explain it in a way that keeps us operational within our societies. Humans seek explanation and fitting it all into a tale allows for a continuous existence, no matter if that story is true in a scientific sense.

Story is everything. It gives us a purpose for what we do. Why do so many homeowners insist on maintaining monoculture green lawns when insects are needed for pollination? While they may agree in principle, the story they are more attached to, is the one that says their property values will decrease if they do not have a uniform lawn. They need to let go of that if they are to become more environmentally conscious citizens.

I am certainly not the first to say that story matters. Professor and author Joseph Campbell crystallized the concept of story and its critical role in his classic book *Power of Myth*. In his series of the same name, reporter Bill Moyers interviewed Campbell. Moyers described Campbell's philosophy of the myths we live by: "Mythology was to him the song of the universe, music so deeply embedded in our collective unconscious that we dance to it, even when we can't name the tune." Campbell was right. We are not only running our lives with stories, we also cannot easily distill them from our histories. We have become even more out of touch as modern society is saturated with 24/7 news cycles that interfere with our ability to examine our stories.

What we collectively believe permits or restricts our actions, good and bad. We began the space program because we believed in its promise. We preserve forests when we believe in their value and we cut them down when we don't. When we value money over everything, we kill the life-giving forces of this planet in pursuit of profit, which won't even matter when the planet loses its ability to support life.

Author Yuval Noah Harari articulates the importance of story in his book, *Sapiens: A Brief History of Humankind.* He also has some interesting explanations for why we are so flawed when it comes to changing our stories. He says it is because during our evolution, we were suddenly thrust into the position of top predator. We made this change quickly without learning how to conduct ourselves. It takes time for a species to understand its niche, and when that niche changes, mistakes are made. The relatively sudden change in our place on the food web has been a challenge to our ability to adapt. To build on Harari's ideas, I believe that although many can see the foolishness of a growth-based narrative, we cannot readily adapt. Once a story gets started and the profiteers take over, the whole story begins to grow like a snowball rolling down a hill. Our global capitalistic systems have invested in the story to dominate the planet's resources, hampering our ability to alter our story to a more sustainable one. Our overpopulated world, and the tremendous growth curve we are experiencing, makes it an even more enormous task to change our ways.

We need a new story. We need several new stories. The ones under which we operate are damaging our lives, our planet, and the innocent species that are going extinct under our watch. If change is to happen, old and dangerous stories must be questioned through the lens of critical thinking, physics and justice. Stories that increase danger, and create suffering, must be dismantled and destroyed. We must defeat them with the truth. We must be relentless in doing so in each new generation and not allow those who work against the truth, often for temporary personal gain, to take hold of the narrative. It is frustrating that justice rarely stands up over time without vigilant protection. Those who control the dominant narratives are invested in them and will fight back at every opportunity. They will erase atrocities out of textbooks and allow only the victors to write history. They will create a segregated world where it is challenging to experience for ourselves the truth about "those people."

Scientists keep warning us about how little time we have left, yet we refuse to listen. I believe the reason is that we have not changed our story about our role in the world. We still hold on to delusional stories that allow us to continue on our paths of destruction. Fairy tales are not just for the young. Our leaders perpetuate them because they are invested in the current story.

Kurt Anderson, in his book *Fantasyland*, theorizes that the United States has always been built on fantasies. Many came to the shores of the United States believing that the streets were literally paved with gold. Anderson believes that Americans are predisposed to believe in magical thinking. The Pilgrims believed Satan himself put the indigenous people in the country to challenge their right to the place. P.T. Barnum raised the bar further only to be out done by Walt Disney and then there are the zealots who claim that Donald Trump was sent to rule the United States by the almighty. It seems logical that all of these people and their beliefs in fantasy were baked into the culture long ago so it should be no surprise that ridiculous ideas like infinite growth in a finite place have so much cultural capital in today's world.

For social and eco-justice to live and breathe, its stories must dominate. We must give these new stories oxygen and set fire to those stories which only serve the rich and powerful.

Imagine for a moment what the world would look like if these stories dominated the airwaves and public discourse:

> Economics is a subset of ecology and must operate accordingly; Jews do not control the world but have been kicked out of more countries than most due to deeply held prejudices; The world must be freed of institutional and individual racism; When women get to decide on their own what they want for their bodies and lives, everyone benefits; Monotheistic religions are questioned for the suffering they permit to happen to non-believers and the inequality of women, and easy access to destructive weapons protects no one and makes us all victims.

The best, most fair and honorable stories need to dominate culture. Women are not property or second-class citizens. This belief needs to squeeze out age-old beliefs that have kept women suffering and from their full potential. Today in the country of Samoa women cannot own property by themselves. Old stories are tied to tradition and power. They are often wrapped up in the dangerous belief that someone's god will be angry if the rules are changed, and hell and damnation await in a place conveniently created to sustain the powerful.

Those who dominate culture never give up without a fight. The first act we must take is to challenge the traditions which cause misery and injustice, or unsustainable practices, or both. Just because your ancestors did it does not mean it should continue. Knowledge and awareness should be our tools for letting go of traditions, which is why critical thinking is so important. The only other tool in our toolbox is destruction. Destruction does work to change narratives, but at a terrible cost.

Catastrophic events, rebellions, and wars can stop narratives in their tracks, but humanity and the Earth have grown weary of this approach. How much better it would be to figure out a way to do it with courage, wisdom, and the creation of progressive and ecologically sound ideas.

Daniel T. Willingham, professor of psychology at the University of Virginia, believes that critical thinking must be taught on top of a foundation of knowledge of subject content. His process has four steps: 1) Identify a list of critical thinking skills for each subject domain; 2) Identify subject matter content for each domain; 3) Plan the sequence in which knowledge and skills should be taught; 4) Plan which knowledge and skill should be revisited across the years. This approach creates constructive critiques desperately needed in a world of assumptions and thoughtless assimilation of old narratives. Humans have a choice: to become more rational or continue to allow emotional attachment to old narratives run and ultimately ruin their lives. We evolved a mammalian brain on top of our reptilian brain. Our mammalian brain needs to kick into gear.

Here are two examples of historically common practices that are no longer a part of our cultural norms. The first, animal sacrifice, was practiced in order to rid one of sins. It is said to have been discontinued by the Jews around the time of the destruction of the temple in Jerusalem in 70 AD. Christians also discontinued it because the need to rid one of sin was no longer needed once Jesus was said to have been sacrificed for everyone's sin. Although a rare tribe or two still consider animal sacrifice a way to appease their gods, for all intents and purposes it is a narrative that is over.

The other, slavery, was practiced in the United States under the widely held belief of white supremacy and the desire for free labor. Once the first slaves were kidnapped, bound, and dragged to America's shores in 1619, they could not escape the brutality of slavery even if they converted to Christianity or if they had white parentage due to rape. It took the bloodiest war in United States history to stop the institution of slavery, though oppression continues in various incarnations from segregation to institutional racism. An estimated 620,000 American soldiers died during the Civil War, more than in all other conflicts combined. We have a horrid record of changing our old stories without a lot of bloodshed.

Movements also have a history in the United States of changing our stories, albeit with a lot of disruption. They are informal and no war is officially declared, but they cost lives and livelihoods as well. The civil rights movement had many casualties besides Martin Luther King Jr. It was littered with suffering and riots, explosions and marches. Fighting for the basic rights guaranteed to all Americans in the Constitution took much more effort than it should have. The white supremacist story has refused to die. We have had so many examples of political, cultural, and social contributions made by Blacks in America , yet some still cling to the notion that whites still reign supreme and have a right to dominate the money and power niches of society while oppressing all who do not share their skin color.

The attachment to ancient traditions and rituals brought our species much success over the years.

But these narratives have run their course and are no longer useful. Now they must be challenged and replaced. The following chapters explore six examples of narratives which need to be changed if we are to ever enjoy a better world.

Chapter 1

From Worship to Wonder

Man is the most insane species. He worships
an invisible god and destroys a visible nature
unaware that this Nature he's destroying is this
god he's worshipping.

—Hubert Reeves

Worship is a sacred cow that gets pardoned endlessly by society. It skips taxation and critical questioning. But worship needs to take a turn in the interrogation seat.

I define worship as a reverence for a deity (or deities) that involves believing all that deity is supposed to have said or commanded, without opportunity to question its relevance--especially among the more orthodox. Worship is the antithesis of critical thinking, our most valuable tool in this challenging life. When we cave to the authority of worship, our critical eye loses focus.

As I write this, people are defying stay- at-home orders meant to flatten the curve of COVID-19's spread. These believers worship the authority of church leaders who say Coronavirus is not a problem despite all of the deaths nationwide. We find ourselves witnessing large groups of believers blindly following a narrative without acknowledging its danger.

During the 2020 pandemic, churches stayed open, or reopened, so people could pray for health while libraries remained closed, a real-time demonstration of our collective priorities. Reports are in: areas where churches were open are now experiencing a surge in COVID-19 cases. Several pastors have died of it. Let us now question the story of worship as it clearly needs to be. Its reign as a sacred cow needs to end.

To figure out why we are prone to worship, we have to dig deep into our evolutionary biology. Our consciousness evolved to a point where we understood that we would eventually die. This has paralyzed our species with fear. To compensate, Homo sapiens adapted in a way that opened the door to religion. Dr. Ajit Varki, from University of California San Diego and author of the book *Denial*, says:

> This is where *Homo sapiens* got lucky. Somewhere in our ancestral history 200,000 years ago, the first modern *Homo sapien* developed an unlikely combination of two maladaptive traits that cancelled each other out: ETOM (human extended theory of mind) and *reality denial*. Reality denial is the neurophysiological basis for humanity's creation of afterlife myths, and it explains why human beings are the only animals who have religions. Reality denial allowed early *Homo sapiens* to convince themselves that their deaths were not permanent, and that their immortal spirits would live on after their physical bodies were terminated.

This explains how we dealt with our fear of mortality. We created stories of immortality. We denied the permanence of death with stories of an afterlife that awaits all good people.

It has, however, outlived its usefulness. Worship has become dangerous. It erases critical thinking and dissolves agency. We are the only species among 4,000 other mammals capable of seeing into the future (see chapter 6), yet worship ties us inextricably to the past. Worship has enabled us to excuse religious institutions and individuals from paying real estate taxes and gives their leadership too much power in our legal system.

Religion is big business too. The fact that churches do not pay real estate taxes in the United States is a slap in the face to the wisdom behind the separation of church and state. Churches represent an economic force in our society, embedded in our economic structure as well as our societal norms. Georgetown University researchers Brian J. and Melissa E. Grimm did an empirical analysis of religion's economic value to United States society. As of 2016, the study's most conservative estimate put the value at $378 billion annually.

Worship is different from wonder, which is needed in order to appreciate the beauty of the natural world. Worship is the devotion to a supernatural being, someone in charge, the rules for which were cemented back when the world knew less about itself. Old stories owe their longevity to our species' devotion to the printed word over present-day evidence. Domination of men over women, for example, began its centuries' long reign in the first words of Genesis.

One of the most violent examples of religion- fueled ideologies is the practice of female genital mutilation (FGM). It comes from a toxic marriage of religion and cultural expectation. It results in the disfigurement and damage of millions of women. It reinforces the story of women remaining loyal to their men by taking away their ability to experience sexual pleasure. It is also deeply embedded in cultural traditions, often as a requirement for marriage to take place. I struggle putting these words on a page, for fear of giving this story legitimacy. This forced loyalty and twisted version of sexual purity sounds horrid to the enlightened mind, yet it is still practiced and entrenched throughout the world. According to the United Nations, FGM is waning, but it still causes far too much misery where women's rights have failed to take hold.

Patriarchy plays a critical role as well. Patriarchy ensures the ongoing diminishment of women. This story continues its arc and grip on young girls who must grow up in rape culture, and with a widespread prejudice that permits men to earn more money and gain more power in the United State. Our government in the United States has yet to elect a woman president, while seventy-five countries have already made women their heads of state. This story needs to find a graveyard fast. It creates power for some and misery for many. It represents a series of narratives which run deep. It's hard to fight back when those who make the rules also make you weak.

Stories are often based on natural phenomena not yet explained. For example, many people once thought that solar eclipses were a sign of impending doom. When science determined them to be part of a natural cycle and nothing more, solar eclipses lost their metaphysical baggage and became regarded as simply an amazing sight.

Other stories aren't so easily debunked. When powerful organizations fold them into their broader narrative, they are more difficult to change. Galileo's discovery that the Earth was not the center of the universe is a great example of what happens when a newly discovered truth collides with a well embedded story stewarded by powerful institutions. Galileo's telescope not only told a new story, but it displaced an old one, one that made us feel significant within the grand scheme of the universe. His discovery threatened the divinity of the human- inhabited Earth and God's role in creation. Many refused to even glimpse through the telescope for fear it might shatter the world as they knew it. This phenomenon is repeated over and over again as modern-day scientists are questioned by those who are threatened by their experiments. Either climate change cannot be caused by humans because that would diminish the power of the god they believe in, or it is real and not to be dealt with because it is fulfilling an end of days prophesy.

Religions of the world provide stories that, at their best, give reasons for good behavior. At their worst, they control, punish, and drain money from those who can afford it least. And for what? To get unproven rewards in a heaven they describe as if they have proof of its existence. Attachment to religious stories is the greatest breeding ground for evil. If a god said to do something, the act doesn't have to be beneficial or just. Oftentimes, when questioning the dominant story starts, sin begins, and life gets worse for a person of faith. Science comes in a distant second to religious dogma.

At the core of much religious dogma is fear. Fear controls followers, be they citizens or parishioners. Interdenominational evangelicals have gained influence over the United States political scene, many supporting our 45th president, because they believe he was sent by their god to rule over them. No matter one's political leanings, we should be frightened to see elections attached to that kind of belief system. It stands as a threat to our representative democracy.

Worshippers share their beliefs often, yet they won't invite criticism. They want everyone to follow their notions of what is right. This is not democratic, nor does it honor the intent of our forefathers, who believed in freedom of religion, separate from the state. Rationality is the better story from which we must govern others and ourselves.

Perhaps the most egregious example of this is the End of Days, or apocalyptic stories. If the end of the world is prescribed by God, why would humans try to alter course? When the deeply religious look at climate change or overpopulation, they may see it as God's plan and not a result of misguided human behavior. What is so dangerous is that what is clearly the act of humans becomes a fatalistic vision of God's puppets. Society is rendered powerless to stop our collective fate.

Minnesota neuroscientist Dr. Shmuel Lissek sheds some light on the appeal of apocalyptic world views. Scientific studies confirm that when a subject is told ahead of time that they will receive a painful shock, it lessens anxiety. Christians take comfort in knowing that the end is near and was built into a system over which they have zero control. Dr. Lissek claims that the doomsday concept evokes an innate and ancient bias in most mammals. "The initial response to any hint of alarm is fear. This is the architecture with which we're built," he says. "Over evolutionary history, organisms with a better-safe-than-sorry approach survive. This mechanism has had consequences for both the body and brain, where the fast-acting amygdala can activate a fearful stress response before 'higher' cortical areas have a chance to assess the situation and respond more rationally."

There may indeed be comfort in knowing that predictions of doom are forecasted in the book of Revelation and that we who are sinners somehow deserve our fate. Believers think it is best to prepare the bunkers rather than fight our fate with policies, protests, or even curiosity.

Atheism is on the rise. "There's absolutely more atheists around today than ever before, both in sheer numbers and as a percentage of humanity," says Phil Zuckerman, a professor of sociology and secular studies at Pitzer College in Claremont, California. According to a Gallup International survey of more than 50,000 people in fifty-seven countries, the number of individuals claiming to be religious fell from seventy-seven to sixty-eight percent between 2005 and 2011, while those who self-identified as atheist rose by three percent–bringing the world's estimated proportion of non-believers to thirteen percent. Yet beliefs in what many would call superstitions are also on the rise. Humans clearly want to believe that life has meaning beyond what science can measure. If this stays in the realm of wonder rather than dogmatic, authoritarian systems, it can be a story beneficial to society. I heard journalist Bari Weiss state in an interview that people have turned their politics into a form of religion, which is not a great development.

The concept of God as one in control of nature has long been challenged. Baruch Spinoza, the Portuguese philosopher born in Amsterdam, said in the 1600's that God was revealed by and a part of nature, not separate from it. Long before that, many indigenous peoples followed and still follow creation stories which place humans within the web of life, not above it. In his paper "Kincentric Ecology: Indigenous Perceptions of the Human-Nature Relationship," Enrique Salmon studies the monotheist ways of dominant culture and how strikingly different they are from those indigenous people.

Salmon, from the Department of Anthropology at Fort Lewis College Colorado states in his abstract that: "Indigenous people view both themselves and nature as part of an extended ecological family that shares ancestry and origins. It is an awareness that life in any environment is viable only when humans view the life surrounding them as kin. The kin, or relatives, include all the natural elements of an ecosystem." If we adopted these types of narratives, they could fundamentally change our relationship to the Earth. If this seems far-fetched, consider the following.

Which of the following are current beliefs from our world's religions?

    a) Sprinkling water on a newborn, if done correctly, can keep the baby from eons of suffering should he or she die prematurely;

    b) Waving a chicken over your head can take away your sins;

    c) [A holy one] climbed a mountain and could see the whole Earth from the mountain peak;

    d) Putting a dirty milk glass and a plate from a roast beef sandwich in the same dishwasher can contaminate your soul;

    e) Invisible supernatural beings reveal themselves in mundane objects like oozing paint or cooking food;

    f) In the end times, [the Holy One's] chosen people will be gathered together in Jackson County, Missouri. Believers can drink poison or get bit by snakes without being harmed.

That was a trick question; they are all beliefs from today's religions. Even educated people perpetuate these stories for a variety of reasons. Traditions die hard. There is no lack of strange beliefs in today's world. David Gee reported in February 2020 that the Hindu leader of the Swaminarayan faith teaches that women who cook while menstruating will be born as a female dog in the next life. These ridiculous claims are believed by those who want gurus to tell them the "truth." But they have real life consequences and must be challenged at every opportunity.

We do need to hang on to stories in order to make society run smoothly, but we need to be careful what those stories are and how deeply they are believed. If you have ever felt uncomfortable inside a house of worship, it is probably because they preach that we are separate from each other, and that only those with the proper pedigree and practice get to go to a fantasy called heaven. We need to stop creating stories for just one elite group. In the case of the Mormon Church, non-Mormons are not even let in the door.

Religion is said to help the world to become more moral, while teaching us how to get along with each other. The partial list below shows how many have died the name of a god. Numbers given based on the geometric mean estimate of reported death tolls as found on Wikipedia in June 2020 except those noted.

- The Crusades: 2,000,000
- Thirty Years War: 5,873,670

- French Wars of Religion: 2,828,427
- Second Sudanese Civil War: 1,414,214
- Lebanese Civil War: 134,164
- Congolese Genocide (King Leopold II): 6,244,998
- Armenian Genocide: 1,095,445
- Rwandan and Burundian Genocides: 1,234,190
- Eighty Years' War: 678,233
- Nigerian Civil War: 2,000,000
- German Peasants' Revolt: 100,000
- First Sudanese Civil War: 1,000,000
- The Holocaust (Jewish and Homosexual Deaths): 5,143,928
- Iraq War: 460,000*
- United States Western Expansion, (Justified by "Manifest Destiny"), also known as the Indigenous Holocaust: 70,000,000
- Atlantic Slave Trade (Justified by Christianity): 10,954,451
- Aztec Human Sacrifice: 316,228
- Spanish Inquisition: 5,000
- TOTAL: 195,035,000 deaths in the name of religion.

The violence perpetuated by today's religions unfortunately is still creating havoc all over the world.

Elaine Pagels, professor of religion at Princeton University, suggests a different way of looking at religion. Perhaps we can use her advice to reinvent how we look at worship. In her book *Why Religion*, she explores how religion's rituals can bring comfort to mourners. Many people enjoy communal singing and bonding. We can still gather and work together through new and more meaningful rituals, absent beliefs and worship. Worship is not the same as ritual. Untethered from deities who are in charge of us, rituals can be a source of harmless, cohesive fun, rather than the fuel of wars.

In 2002, I handed in my doctoral dissertation and my committee chair told me to take a vacation and relax. I chose to leave the country without a passport. I went to Hopi Nation, located in the three mesas region of Arizona. The Hopi people were in the midst of preparing for their spring festival. It was three weeks long and involved the whole community in food and ritual preparation. As an outsider, I saw that the goal of their rituals was to have fun and honor their ancestors. I never felt like I didn't belong.

In 2005, Greg Epstein, an author and humanist chaplain at Harvard University and the Massachusetts Institute of Technology, tried to answer a fundamental question with his book, *Can We Be Good Without God*. Without an omnipotent god in our universe, how would society hold together? How would we know how to behave? He professes that one can and should live a moral life, one that is devoted to "alleviating unnecessary suffering and promoting human flourishing or dignity" and that a meaningful life is a moral one. One does not need a god to be moral.

Religion, and even its counterpart, humanism, tend to be almost universally and understandably human-centric, or anthropocentric. Humans are given permission to behave in certain ways toward each other and toward other creatures by religious dogma or one's own sense of justice. They are both rather weak in their acknowledgement of life's interconnected nature. The destruction of the Earth often takes a back seat to the atrocities we perform on one another. These narratives form the way we tell the stories of current events. A quick look at any number of newscasts reveals that our priorities are the human condition. When a forest burns, we focus on how many homes burned before we mention wildlife or the carbon released into the atmosphere. Murders and accidents, job markets and the foibles of politicians fill the airwaves, allowing our anthropocentric worldview to crystallize and manifest itself in the world.

The good news is that we do not have to reinvent the wheel. Indigenous people altered their landscapes, but in ways that sustained them for tens of thousands of years before our stories of dominion trampled them. We need our stories to emulate the ones that see sustainability as an integral part of the story of human dependence on wildlife. It is one that already has a proven track record. It doesn't take a very deep dive into current events to see that we need to change this story immediately.

In this chapter, I have focused most of my attention on the concept of religious worship, but it also applies to celebrity worship. We turn movie stars, reality show contestants, musicians, politicians and athletes into gods. They often disappoint us because of it. They make us disappointed in ourselves as well. We compare our self-worth to their wealth and talents, thereby diminishing ourselves. Celebrity worship means that they lose perspective, autonomy and any kind of privacy beyond their mansion walls. There is a reason so many celebrities are in rehab or die tragically from substance abuse. Even worse, some are or should be in prison because they believed that their status made them invincible to the rule of law. The rich and famous need a connection to reality, and they cannot live up to the pedestal we place them on. Only when we see ourselves as all having value can we move in a much better direction.

Chapter 2

From Greed to Need

Greed is a fat demon and whatever you feed
it is never enough.

—Janwillem van de Wetering

As I write, Coronavirus is showing our economy for the Ponzi scheme that it is. We are tied into a system that is collapsing around us. While I began this book long before the pandemic took hold, it makes for a perfect example of an old story failing us. Our economy only serves the very rich and now we can only hope to get enough basic supplies. We hang on to our loved ones through Zoom meetings and, if we dare, socially distanced outdoor gatherings. We can't even touch each other anymore because we might make each other sick.

It is a surreal time in human history, but those of us who have been involved in global ecology are not surprised, just saddened. No matter how many films my colleagues make, no matter how many books we write, only this virus has caught our collective attention. Yet here I am writing another book because it is my only tool to show that our stories have been wrong all along and must change. The pandemic has revealed to a larger audience the extent of our flawed unsustainable economic system.

Before COVID-19, I had grown weary of being treated as just an undervalued consumer in a consumer culture brought to you by our untethered capitalist system. Money is our motivation and buying and selling is our game. Everything is boiled down to a sales pitch. Want to learn about the latest health gimmick? First you have to listen to a nauseatingly long YouTube video at the end of which you have to send in for a book. Politicians sell us the magic beans of never-ending growth and we buy it because it is the only story that we know. We believe their false promises about how they will grow jobs and the economy because we think we know it must happen. Limits to growth just aren't on the table and wouldn't sell well anyway.

Merchants sell us products by selling us youth, sex, and fame. All of it diminishes our value as citizens and discourages any relationship to the true value of being a human in our society. We are consumers, respected only when we take out our credit cards. The merry-go-rounds of our rapid-fire lives are the fuel that burns to keep our growth-based economy afloat. Meanwhile, the Earth is paying the real price.

According to psychologist Dr. Gabor Maté, capitalism makes us sick. It creates chronic stress due to the pressure to produce and succeed. This makes us chronically ill. People try to keep up with their neighbors by grinding away at jobs they don't like to buy stuff they don't need. George Carlin famously took a look at the stuff Americans buy to get happy, and pointed out that the storage industry profits as we keep buying more space to keep our stuff that never really makes us any happier. Social media has added a layer to this phenomenon. Now we can binge-scroll through our Instagram feed to see our friends supposedly find their happiness through new toys, and we almost pass out from the stress and futility of it all.

Stuart Scott, founder and executive director of Scientists Warning Foundation, has devoted his life to alerting the world to the way our current global economic systems make the Earth sick. Behind many of our problems, according to Scott, are limitless growth and neoclassical economics. Our multinational global economy rests on a false premise. The boardrooms and C-suites of Wall Street are full of empty suits. They either believe in limitless growth on a limited planet or choose to ignore its obvious result.

Greed can be divided into two types: individual greed and corporate greed. We often badmouth individual greed as sinful and wasteful, but corporate greed is exponentially worse, and it bears more responsibility for the accelerated rate of humanity's global destruction and the crippling of our society.

Merriam-Webster defines greed as "a selfish and excessive desire for more of something, such as money, than is needed." Worship of money has corrupted our society, but power is its evil twin; you rarely see one without the other.

The lottery, like all gambling, sells the fantasy that you could win a huge payout, but the chances are extremely slim. According to Steve Spring of Market Watch, you are 400 times more likely to be hit by lightning than to win the lottery. The lottery sells the dream of wealth and the promise of happiness when you finally find the gold at the end of the rainbow.

A classic 1978 study by Brickman, Coates and Janoff-Bulman, and published in the Journal of Personality and Social Psychology, compared twenty-two lottery winners with twenty-two people who didn't win any money. They also studied twenty-nine people who were paralyzed in accidents. They found that winning the lottery didn't increase long-term happiness and being paralyzed in an accident only left people slightly less unhappy than those who had not been in an accident. Researchers concluded that people have a happiness set point, and even life-changing events do not alter it significantly. In other words, money doesn't buy happiness, but our society keeps the myth alive. Wendell Berry, from his perch in Kentucky as a small acreage farmer, wishes we would consider an alternative to the rampant capitalism that is conquering the world. Berry suggests the creation of a new Emancipation Proclamation to freedom from the tyranny of corporations. Capitalism as a tool of the tyrannical subjugation wielded by credit card companies, banks, and health care corporations is a story that, if told with greater regularity, could begin to eat away at the myth that this system benefits us enough to warrant its continuation.

The Center for the Advancement of the Steady State Economy (CASSE) believes the following: From their website "Economic sustainability requires a steady state economy with stabilized population and a rigorous labor force working in tandem with appropriate technology."

I applaud efforts to offer alternatives to our current global predatory unregulated capitalism. But CASSE's call for stabilized population raises the question: At what number do we stabilize? The unfortunate reality is that our world is already overpopulated, and that even a steady state economy at eight, nine or ten billion is not sustainable. We need a new system coupled with a reduced population, achieved in the most humane ways possible of course.

It is impossible to divorce the economy from the number of people it is supposed to serve. According to Global Footprint Network, globally sustainable numbers are somewhere around one-two billion depending on the level of consumption. That translates to roughly 150 million in the United States depending on our level of consumption and the state of our remaining resources like fresh water. As our consumerism rises and our carbon footprint increases, I would argue that the sustainable human population count is much lower than that. If environmental groups put population clocks on their websites, and if ecology classes taught facts about the unsustainability of population growth, more of us would know the significance of our situation as we near eight billion worldwide and 330 million in the United States in 2020.

Today's capitalist system encourages millionaires to become billionaires and billionaires to become multi-billionaires. This is all done at the expense of the poor working class and ever shrinking middle classes. When the rich donate to political campaigns, they ask for tax and other favors in return. This has fostered a world with pro-rich tax loopholes.

Capitalism and all systems to date, essentially take natural resources and converts them into monetary wealth. This is inherently unsustainable, because natural resources, when converted into money, always add pollution and waste into the earth's closed system. Today we live in an elevated system of outrageous growth because we have now become much more of a plutocracy than a democracy.

This super inflated environment of greed is exemplified by Amazon CEO, Jeff Bezos, who can now brag that he has become the world's first trillionaire. In our world where greed rules the day, he can accumulate his billions while refusing to provide health insurance or offer decent wages to his workers. This system not only fails the majority of Americans, but it is morally reprehensible. Plutocracy, and taxation of the least advantaged to benefit the rich, led to the first shot of the Revolutionary War. the American reality today is arguably a far cry from the democracy our forefathers had in mind.

Chapter 3

From Limitless to Limited

Your almost incredible surge of growth from one
billion in 1804 to seven billion in 2011 (just 207
years) seems perfectly unremarkable to you, yet
it's precisely this surge that has made you the
enemy of all life on this planet.

—From *Ishmael* by Daniel Quinn

If the Earth did not have limits, we could easily keep growing by eighty million people a year. If our modern post-industrial world's demand for resources like rare earth minerals did not create pollution and greenhouse gases, there would be no reason to stop what we are doing.

But they do.

There are renewable resources, nonrenewable resources and perpetual resources. The concept of renewable resources is misleading. While trees can be replanted and water can recharge, if they are consumed too rapidly, they will run out too. Fish are renewable resources up until our demand exceeds their ability to reproduce. We have already seen huge declines in fish populations, all the more exacerbated by warming waters.

Nonrenewable minerals were formed billions of years ago. They are diminishing each day with our ever- growing demand. Many argue about their abundance, but more importantly, their extraction causes huge problems to the environment. The process requires large amounts of water and leaves behind deeply embedded toxicity. "To provide most of our power through renewables would take hundreds of times the amount of rare earth metals that we are mining today," said Thomas Graedel, professor of Industrial Ecology at the School of Forestry and Environmental Studies at Yale University. Wildlife suffers greatly from our ability to conquer their world. Our ingenuity, combined with our need to live at the top of the food chain, creates a pathway to extinction for many species. Our greed plays a role here as well. To lighten our pressure on the planet's resources and create a way for our species to continue, we must have fewer of us. Before we can discuss how our human numbers overwhelm our resources, we **must** prove that technology is not our savior. That is the default argument when the overpopulation problem is brought up. The first argument against technology-as-savior is that energy, and all it does for us, is not the only principle we need to survive on the planet. We need fresh clean water, air and open space and room for the wild animals of our ecosystem that we depend on, especially the insects.

All human endeavors consume resources, especially during the shift from one form of technology to another. No one has illustrated this better than Jeff Gibbs in his film *Planet of the Humans*. Together with author and researcher Ozzie Zehner, they make a case for why green technologies cannot live up to their promises. To trust technology to save us, is to ignore the total impact of humans as well as the reality of physics. Humans depend on so many resources and the more technologically advanced we are the more resources we need. Conversions to non-carbon producing energy sources won't yield the energy we have convinced ourselves we need.

Long before I saw this groundbreaking film, I had worried that even with a miraculous discovery of a perfect source of energy we would be in deep trouble. A cheap and magically clean energy source will only be a greater excuse to continue pillaging this planet. We look for a greener way to power our bulldozers when what we need are fewer bulldozers.

Christopher Clugston dips our technology hopes in cold water when he tells us in his book, *Scarcity: Humanity's Final Chapter* that technology relies on NNR'S (Non-renewable natural resources) including oil, metal and minerals, fifty-seven of them to be exact. These are the building blocks of technology and as we grow in numbers and desire for more devices, we are rendering them more and more scarce.

He says, "Our industrial lifestyle paradigm is enabled by nonrenewable natural resources (NNRs)—energy resources, metals, and minerals. Both the support infrastructure within industrialized nations and the raw material inputs into industrialized economies consist almost entirely of NNRs; NNRs are the primary sources of the tremendous wealth surpluses required to perpetuate industrialized societies. As a case in point, the percentage of NNR inputs into the United States economy increased from less than ten percent in the year 1800, which corresponds roughly with the inception of the American industrial revolution, to approximately ninety-five percent today." He goes on to say that we have increased our NNR usage from 4 million to seven billion tons since 1800. This demand of limited resources cannot continue indefinitely and points out the physical flaws in the argument that technology is the answer to perpetual growth.

The argument, made so well in the *Planet of the Humans* documentary, is that humans are a force, especially modern humans. Each invention we make, whether it is well intended or not, works against the natural world on which we depend. Every time we invent something to further our well-being, we extract resources and leave waste and destruction in our wake. Now multiply that by nearly eight billion of us and it can only spell trouble.

At first blush, it seems ludicrous to discuss overpopulation in the time of Coronavirus, so let me put this into a broader context. Over the years, my scholarly overpopulation colleagues and I have tried to get the attention of leaders, and the public, to warn of the chaos headed our way when our numbers completely overwhelm our resources. We have warned about the collective impact on everything from climate change to water scarcity. Many of us have also cautioned about the false promise of housing-based solutions. The answer to our growing population will not be found in increasing residential density. Mass transit and more apartments have been our 'green' answers to solving the overpopulation problem. The negative impacts of increased crime, traffic, pollution, anonymity, and the stress on our localized water resources were not strong enough consequences to persuade our targeted audiences. Now that we are struggling to enforce social distancing guidelines, we can see how public policies brought about our own doom.

Our whole world is turning upside down. We are living in the most surreal and ironic of times. But it is also an opportunity to rethink how we warehouse people to solve the problem of growth. We have quickly learned that density helps to spread infection. This knowledge must now translate into future policies that will improve our safety. As environmental advocate Gary Wockner, Ph.D., wrote in the Boulder Daily Camera: "The verdict is in—'density' is the primary cause of the transmission of the Coronavirus and a significant contributor to the death of people infected. As we come out of the Coronavirus lockdown, stopping the densification of our cities, including Boulder, should be goal No. 1 of public policy."

The only other way to accommodate growth is to sprawl over open land. This has all kinds of other bad results including loss of wildlife, destruction of agricultural soils and increased traffic among others. If we can't go up, we must go out. It is an environmental Sophie's choice, for which there is no good answer, except a set of policies which would discourage growth under a new sustainable narrative.

Addressing overpopulation is a great protection plan for the planet and its inhabitants. We would protect ourselves from loss of wildlife habitat, loss of water and mineral resources, excess carbon in the atmosphere, more traffic, and more rapid-spreading deadly viruses.

It's a simple idea; one cannot demand limitless resources from a limited place. As soon as we broke the chains of gravity, we could see the boundaries of our spherical planet. Satellite views of the Earth sealed the deal for scientists, but old stories of a limitless landscape persist. They favor expansionist activities, benefiting those who profit when the Dow Industrial and the SP 500's numbers go up.

Mahatma Gandhi once said that the Earth can handle our needs but not our greed. That used to be true, but no longer. Just the daily needs of 7.8 billion of us are too much, and we are growing by over eighty million each year. In Gandhi's defense, he was born in 1869 when the globe hadn't even reached 1.6 billion. Though many politicians and even environmental groups find it convenient to ignore the impact of nearly the seven billion consumers that have been added since, the time to stop ignoring the force of overpopulation is yesterday. We need to reverse these stories. Even one billion is a hard quantity to comprehend. For reference, one billion seconds is equal to 240 years. Ask someone to snap their fingers every second one billion times and you will exceed their life expectancy by approximately 160 years. We need to name the main reasons why overpopulation is here and knocking at our door so loudly. If we can come to terms with how we got here, only then can we begin to untangle ourselves from its deadly grip. To keep it simplified while remaining truthful, think of the overpopulation issue like a four-legged iron stool squishing the Earth and its potential for supporting all life forms, not just us. All of the legs of the oppressive stool of overpopulation work together to create the mess, yet they do not all get the attention they need.

First, let's talk about Total Fertility Rate. That is a key metric used by groups like World Population Balance (WPB) to target as their focus. Because each child in the developed world has a carbon footprint calculated at fifty-six tons in an average lifetime, having small families is a necessary goal. In 2020, WPB launched a campaign to get people to consider the benefits of reducing family size to one child per family in order to protect the planet. In the 1970's, back when population was discussed more openly, the group Zero Population Growth recommended that families stop at two. Because there are so many more people on the planet now, the momentum baked into the system means that even at two child families, we will grow to at least nine billion. The second leg of the overpopulation stool is neo-classical capitalism, as addressed in the Greed to Need chapter. It has contributed more than its fair share to the overall framework we use to justify our growing numbers. Our fossil fuel powered neo-classical economic system has enabled us to convert cheap energy calories into growing food and manufacturing products, which in turn requires more growth to maintain itself in a Ponzi scheme of never-ending growth. The proliferation of nuclear power, coal, and natural gas keep us growing our footprint by fueling our ability to grow food and produce higher quantities. New sources of energy, even if they were viable, would just keep the machinery running that encourages more population growth which can never buy us more clean air, fresh water and open land.

No one has confronted our faulty growth story better than my colleague, filmmaker Dave Gardner. He took on the incredible task of dismantling our addiction to growth through many interviews with environmental experts. Gardner tried to focus our attention on the policies that promote growth in the US, the country leading the world in a pro-growth narrative. His documentary film *Growthbusters* brings up many facts about growth promotion. Cities get more federal money for development of roads and bridges when their populations grow. Families get more tax deductions with each child born to them. Wall Street bells ring with glee when companies merge to form and expand multi-national corporations. Those entities then have more capital to fund the chewing up of our limited resources.

The third leg of the overpopulation stool is the impact immigration and migration have on our growth. In today's climate, they are addressed by only the bravest among us. Caught in a politically incorrect trap of those who claim injustice before any argument is made, it remains a hazardous zone where few dare to tread. Immigration policies are a given government's permission slip to welcome in new residents who become citizens. Humans move around the globe for better education and economic opportunities, often, but not always, out of desperation. Immigration policies control the numbers of refugees and other immigrants that contribute to a country's growth. In the case of the US, immigration is currently responsible for two-thirds of growth. Population must be controlled country by country, for that is how and where policies are made. In the US, it is ironically both the easiest aspect of growth to control and the one surrounded by so much controversy. Understandably, people who have made a better life for themselves in this country of immigrants want to bring over their loved ones and to keep reproducing according to their cultural and religious traditions. The problem is that this cannot continue if we want to prevent the problems that come with overcrowding and resource scarcity.

I am a proud granddaughter of Russian Jewish immigrants who were able to get into the United States in the 1920's in order to escape the Bolshevik Revolution and the antisemitism it fostered. Our legal immigration policies back then aimed to reign in immigration due to a zeitgeist of xenophobia and prejudice. It is so ironic and backwards that the United States then had only 110 million people living within our borders then and yet immigration limits were as low as 150,000. My great uncle, who I got to meet only once when I was thirteen, did not make it into those quotas, which is why I now have cousins living in Argentina. Now that our population is nearing 330 million, our legal immigration is over a million people per year. How insane is it that the larger our population is, the more we legally welcome into our country? It demonstrates that other, more dominant narratives are in place. We have told the story that we must do what it says on the Statue of Liberty. According to our collective myth, we must open our lands and hearts to people in need. To do otherwise is to be less than American. No matter that the gift from France in 1881 was about liberty. Liberty enlightening the world was meant to be a signal to people around the world to rise up and establish their own liberal republics. The poem by Emma Lazarus was added years later, changing the intention completely. It solidified a story that we are a caring people and to reject desperate people is not who we are. But we cannot continue to sell the American Dream to everyone. The natural world will not allow it.

Since the gift of this iconic statue, the United States has gained 280 million changing the landscape in ways that are no longer sustainable if we want enough water, wildlife, open space, low traffic highways and a good quality of life.

Some have challenged this argument, saying that we are silly to criticize immigration because it is a global problem. But populations are produced locally, and we will make no progress with population issues until we de-globalize them. Unfortunately, many Americans seem to believe that our nation can solve everyone else's population problems. Now we have another political conundrum, if we argue for the need to limit immigration because of the ecological limits of the United States we are painted as siding with those with sinister racist motives. In our current climate, our population story in the United States and elsewhere permits no nuanced conversation and instant labeling is never good for progress.

In today's unfortunate cancel culture mentality, the interest to protect and preserve America, or any developed nation by keeping a line on however growth is happening locally is deemed racist without a trial. I know of people who are losing their positions at universities just for wanting to have a fair and ecologically based discussion on these policies. My support of them begins with a definition of a racist. If you look up the definition of a racist you will see that it is, "the belief that different races possess distinct characteristics, abilities, or qualities, especially so as to distinguish them as inferior or superior to one another." A newer definition of "racism" is "a political or social system founded on racism."

There are still many in our society and in our government who not only believe this but they make laws that continue to embed racism into our systems. Those who do believe in equality must fight for laws to protect their liberties and even the right not to be persecuted in the workplace. We must fight for the eradication of racist ideology everywhere but especially in the US. What we must NOT do is call out racism when it is not. We cannot call everyone a racist for having thoughts and ideas that are either new to us or relatively unexamined. We cannot have people dismissed or fired because we THINK they are racist. I am upset by the very notion of racists and the harm they can and do cause. I think what happens is that those who think and operate on a macro level get in trouble with those who are using a vacuum cleaner to rid the world of suspected racists rather than truly examine them with a more appropriate fine-tooth comb. That vacuum cleaner is violating one of the most sacred laws of our justice system, that one is innocent until proven guilty. In today's world just a whisper is needed to throw someone's career away, reminiscent of the McCarthy era when it was thought communism was lurking everywhere especially in Hollywood.

Population activists are committed to the health of our environment. We know that to do so we must work to stabilize our population. But the minute people hear certain trigger words a lot of assumptions are made. Population is just such a word; I know because as a fellow activist on this issue I have been accused of racism as well. Actually, the opposite is true. The already marginalized will hurt first and most as our numbers increase and we have to provide the infrastructure and resources to support them. The already rich and privileged will be able to protect themselves longer from the harm caused by the over demand of our limited resources.

We try hard to make policy makers see how our policies of untethered growth hurt everything from our water supplies to wildlife and our ability to support those within our borders already. To work to dismiss intelligent and out of the box thinkers and advocates for the kind of world we all want and need to live in, does not serve our collective need to eradicate racism. It only serves our dysfunctional need to say we have done something in a world that needs so much fixing. I request that those calling for the canceling of anyone involved in population stabilization actually read their work and become familiar with macro level environmental thinking. To continue to ignore what we are really saying is to harm the already disadvantaged among us. Environmental ills aggravate inequality. Scarcity is felt first by those without enough. Scarcity is not alleviated by having a larger population, it is exacerbated by it. So, to listen to those who have spent their careers studying these issues is to potentially help those we should be caring about the most. There is an Emmy award winning short documentary called, *Tashi and the Monk from Pilgrim Films*, which illustrates the upstream thinking I am talking about here. The Buddhist monk featured in the film, himself an orphan, decides to create a loving community and take in orphans so that they can be nurtured and educated. He wants them to have promising, loving lives. He soon becomes a father figure to ninety children. At one point in the film he turns away an obviously needy boy. At first viewers think he is heartless by turning him away, but it soon becomes clear that the community is full to the brim. There are no more beds and the staff complain about not being able to give each child the food, space and attention they need already. They beg the monk to please not allow in anymore children or the children they are trying to help will suffer. The monk is not a harsh child hater, he is a loving man faced with hard decisions. Those who are holding up a mirror and showing the breach of the carrying capacity of the United States and many other countries are not evil either. We must not shoot the messenger; we must give a platform to those trying to make us see what is difficult to grasp giving our current narratives.

Only when our dominant story becomes about preventing chaos and suffering can we begin to have civil conversations about where most of our growth is coming from in the US. It's difficult to bring up our legal immigration policies, yet so much growth of our population can be attributed to acts of Congress that welcome in more newcomers than our environment and economy can handle. According to the Pew Research Center, if our current immigration policies remain in place, 100 million people will be added to the United States population by 2065, seventy-five million will be the result of immigration.

To continue to knock only on the door of total fertility rate when the rate in the United States is now down to 1.7 children per women is outdated when over eighty-eight percent of our population growth in the United States can be attributed to our immigration policies. According the Global Footprint network the United States is way overpopulated relative to its resources, as many developed countries are. We need to be somewhere around 150 million not the 330 million we now must find all sorts of resources for in an ever-stressed world. Many point to our ridiculous consumption habits as the evildoer. No doubt our love affair with large cars, huge homes and eye-popping shopping habits are owed much of the blame. But those have been in the bullseye of shame for a long time with little results. At a certain point just 330 million people trying to get to work, buy food and even flush a toilet is enough consumption to put us over the edge.

The fourth leg of the stool, increasing longevity and decreasing mortality, is probably the most difficult to address and the hardest to unpack. Our success at decreasing infant mortality and increasing nutrition has drastically increased life expectancy, which has many personal benefits but increases the use of the planet's resources. Hunter gatherer statistics are gathered from a few well studied indigenous groups, specifically the !Kung, Aché, Agta, Hadza, and Hiwi. Their research shows that approximately sixty percent of hunter-gatherer children live to age of only fifteen. Only sixty-eight percent of those will live to the ripe old age of forty-five. If they make it to forty-five then they can make it to sixty-five. In today's world longevity is much higher, 78.6 years in the United States and eighty-five in Japan for example. We have a biological imperative and a moral one to promote our species, but we may indeed be doing too good of a job.

Looking at humans in the same light as other species will reveal that we are removing all the ways nature is trying to keep us in bounds, to the ultimate peril of us all. We need to have civil discussions about all aspects of our takeover of the planet, even considering the grim reality that our impulses to increase our lifespans and solve our health problems may set us up for a big and certain fall.

This effort needs to be heard even more now as we wake up in this new world of uncertainty. It is not inhumane to have these discussions even now that we are in desperate search of a vaccine to cure COVID-19.

Animals must live within boundaries which have been set by the laws of physics. The food pyramid is built in such a way that each trophic level has to remain within its population boundaries. The most powerful predators cannot be the most numerous. Imagine a world where there are more owls than the skunks they eat. Now imagine a world where there are more skunks than grasshoppers. The numbers at each trophic level must make ecological sense. Nowhere in the wild world can we find examples where the top predator is also the most numerous. A sharp increase in sharks, for example, would mean that they would soon overwhelm the fish they eat, and sharks would experience a huge die-off as they run out of food.

Whenever nature's natural checks and balances are thwarted, something goes awry. Take the macaque monkeys of Thailand. In this primarily Buddhist country, the dominant story is that it is considered good karma to treat animals kindly. The story continues that monkeys are also very holy. So instead of disease and starvation, which would limit the overpopulation of macaques in a natural way, people feed them high quality food, believing they are increasing their karma. The only thing they are increasing is the population of macaques who now rule the streets of major cities. They steal food, hats and sunglasses from tourists and even send their adjacent human neighbors to the emergency room when their bites and scratches create worry of possible rabies.

I know It is hard to look at humans at a biological level. Our cultures, influenced by our monotheistic religions, have taught us that we are special. But if we can move upstream and see that we are indeed a part of the natural world and subject to its laws, we could have a much better collective future. Our pro- human policies of stopping every disaster that comes our way is helping to create a world totally overrun by us, its top predator. By disobeying a basic law of nature, we interfere with nature's natural set points.

To bring corn to deer who are starving in a northern Minnesota landscape during a particularly snowy winter is to make sure that they will starve in greater numbers in the future. Those laws apply to us too. Fires, storms, diseases, and lack of nutritious food limit the number of species in any given region. If nothing periodically thinned out populations, their growing numbers would eventually destroy their environment and create a greater tragedy when thousands if not millions more suffer and die.

Harsh, arid landscapes were never meant to support a lot of people. Roaming bands of nomads can handle low water supplies and sandy deserts. Cities built on poor soils in areas of low rainfall will not last for long and will destroy untold wildlife in the process.

I have often said to surprised and disapproving audiences that when you feed starving children, you get more starving children, unless the root problem of overpopulation is also addressed. Daniel Quinn, through his Ishmael series and in many works since then, says that when we ONLY feed the starving, we ensure that there will be more starving next year, as food availability is the greatest indicator of reproduction. Without food, people do not reproduce. With it, they will.

To try to offer birth control is expensive and challenging to implement in countries structurally and religiously opposed to it. The Bill and Melinda Gates Foundation is devoted to solving poverty and generously gives away billions to poor farmers and millions to family planning each year as two of the most philanthropic donors in the world. It just important to understand the relationship between the donation of food and birth control.

To temporarily stop famines is to create a future of greater scarcity. It seems harsh and unfeasible in a world where we universally believe in curing all diseases and sending thousands of pounds of grain to war-torn and famine stressed areas. But, again, from the most distant overarching view, a species perspective, it truly is creating an insurmountable problem down the road as more survive, reproduce and need even more of the earth's limited resources.

Cape Town, South Africa, is running out of water for its population of millions. Only the rich get access to bottled water. The poor are scrounging. Many blame distribution and politicians for falling down on the job. It's hard to find any news story willing to say that Cape Town has 4 million more people to provide for since the 1950's. The United States Agency for International Development (USAID) does have a multi- agency program for family planning. It struggles to bring access to women who desire smaller families because the hurdles are deeply cultural. USAID and other institutions of global health are simultaneously working to help people struggling with poverty, war, and disease. While saving people from the ravages of malaria, AIDS, and other horrific diseases, it is important to calculate what the long-term effects are of helping people avoid death in places which are already experiencing water and food shortages. With this perspective in place, people around the globe could better plan for a more viable future. Measuring how many people can survive in drought-stricken areas exacerbated by climate change, without additional help from overseas, would be a beneficial first step. Remember that preventing suffering is the goal, and suffering is not prevented when we artificially prop up human numbers in areas not able to support them in the long run. When we move away from a human-centric story, we can start to hear the truth about the weight of human overpopulation and all of its causes on the planet.

The story of overpopulation should be embraced by all organizations with an environmental mission. Greenpeace International has a video out (circa 2020) titled, "Countdown to Destruction," which points to the obvious evils of agri-business and its roll in destroying the rainforest. They manage to mention everything BUT overpopulation.

Unfortunately for all of us, it has been deliberately ignored on so many occasions and by so many organizations. Only the bravest will have me or my colleagues come to speak at their conferences. Take the Earth Organization for Sustainability. A quick perusal of their website shows a stunning lack of concern for human numbers. According to them, three criteria must be realized to achieve sustainability globally: 1) A global resource survey: We need to know how much we can take from the Earth and where before we start to use resources, in order to know if we are using more than the biosphere can cope with in any area; 2) A circular economy: In order to minimize our resource usage and optimize our utility, we must form our economy in such a way that we reduce waste, recycle everything that could be recycled, and manage our resources consciously and intelligently; 3) A guaranteed basic income: All human beings deserve to live, to pursue their creativity and to form meaningful lives. We cannot build a sustainable civilization if all humans do not have access to shelter, food, drinking water and energy. They make no mention of how many humans will be able to accomplish this, or that we are also growing by more than one million a week on a planet so full of our pollution and thirst for even the most basic of resources.

World Wildlife Fund, (WWF) along with many others, has the same problem. It was criticized by British environmentalist Jonathan Porritt in 2018 for looking only at consumption, a seemingly safer zone in which to tackle how we are destroying the planet with our habits. "In other words, it's all about over- consumption–as if consumption somehow has nothing to do with the number of people doing the consuming! As if the number of middle-class consumers isn't increasing year on year, as many of the world's developing and emerging countries improve the material living standards of more and more of their citizens." Sir Peter Scott, one of its founders, reflected on WWF's failure to save one single species due to its lack of focus on overpopulation.

Are there problems that will arise when a growth-based world switches over to a degrowth world? Most certainly there will be very difficult adjustments, but compared to what? We can switch to a different economic system, a new way of raising smaller families and caring for our elderly. We can't afford to resist this opportunity to re-examine our unsustainable systems and rethink them from their very core assumptions. Most of these assumptions include a total disregard about how our ecological systems work.

Jonathan Porritt, as the new president of UK-based charity Population Matters, further expressed his frustration at the cowardice of organizations like WWF, much like I have done in essays and in my previous book, *Move Upstream*. "I'm not just sad at this cumulative betrayal of the natural world: I'm seething with anger at the craven cowardice that lies behind it. For so many conservationists and environmentalists today, opting for an easy life by avoiding the controversies associated with population is now the default option."

We know that mandating physical education in the 1960's made a huge impact on our country. Mandating ecological education in high schools throughout the country and the world could have the same positive effect. This is not the same as "sustainable development," and must be taught in a way that empowers students to create a new way of being on the planet. Those two words put together are as meaningless as "jumbo shrimp" or "smart growth." As the late Albert Bartlett, Emeritus Professor of Physics at the University of Colorado at Boulder said, "Smart growth destroys the environment. Dumb growth destroys the environment. The only difference is that smart growth does it with good taste." Being dishonest about how ecology works has only hurt us.

My friend and colleague, João L. R. Abegao, wrote a paper published online on March 10, 2010, called "Internalizing Collapse: A window to the end of civilization." Here is a nugget from his deeply enlightened work: 'It should come as no surprise that Homo sapiens is quickly becoming the harbinger of its own demise, due to a mixture of increased economic output and simple biological rules, which is to say that humanity's appetite has grown too large to be sustained in a prolonged sense."

Reason must rule. It needs to become our most dominant story and told in ways we can hear it. It cannot continue to be dictated by our emotions for those who are desperate for a new life. Neither can it continue to be falsely used to support the mistreatment of those who are trying to immigrate, with or without going through the legal process. It cannot be dictated by hatred for any ethnic and religious groups. It must solely be based on our current ecological limits and future ability to provide for our citizens. When our climate crisis is added to the mix, the situation becomes even more important to examine. All growing regions are in jeopardy as rainfalls are coming in deluges and droughts will become more frequent. This is a situation where the addition of more people is not helping anyone.

COVID-19 may be our greatest teacher if we don't abandon the lesson out of justified fear. To tackle overpopulation is to also help prevent future pandemics. In a bold essay published on April 20, 2020 in the *South China Morning Post* magazine, writer Stephen McCarty takes us to task for not taking responsibility for how we are to blame for the way viruses spread:

> Think COVID-19 is animal in origin? Think again. It's anthropogenic: caused by human activity. The pandemic, which won't be the last zoonotic disease to cut a swathe through Homo sapiens, is a human overpopulation problem. You don't have to live in Mong Kok to know there are too many of us. There are now 7.8 billion people on the planet; the United Nations predicts the population will reach 9.8 billion by 2050 and 11.2 billion by 2100 at the current rate of proliferation.

Our own proliferation is our enemy, globally and locally. Wrestling with it in all of its complexities with an open mind and compassionate heart is our current and tremendous challenge. It remains a desperate call to action which needs to begin with an end to our love affair with our story of limitlessness.

The iron stool of overpopulation is oppressive. It weighs us down with its harsh lesson of limits. Understanding how we grew from millions to multiple billions is important so that we may grapple with how to crawl back from what many call the cliff of collapse. It is incredibly overwhelming to look at just one of these legs let alone look at all of them, but they all play a role and to address one without others is a recipe for failure. Talk of the evils of de-population and the delusional ability of the United States to handle a billion people is bubbling up in the literature. We must respond with the efficacy of numbers. We are approximately 5.5 billion in overshoot now. News of decreasing population is to be greeted with a sigh of relief as we will have more time to regroup and rethink our relationship to spaceship Earth.

The only thing that seems to be limitless is our creativity. We must focus our creativity on a way to live within the biocapacity of our earth.

Chapter 4

From Synthetic to the Natural

It seems to me that the natural world is the
greatest source of excitement, the greatest
source of visual beauty, the greatest source of
intellectual interest, it is the greatest source of so
much in life that makes life worth living.

—Sir David Attenborough

Walking is a natural form of exercise. We do not need fancy equipment or expensive health club memberships to get out and take advantage of the elements. Indeed, in the time of COVID-19 shutdowns, walking has been rediscovered because our gyms have been closed. We need to rediscover the natural world, as we have become too comfortable with the synthetic world and its promise of making life easier. Our machines give us information on demand. We talk to our remote controls. Our cars are going driverless. Much of our agency, our skill sets, and our connection to the way the world works is lost in the balance. We evolved in the three-dimensional world of wind, forest, prairie and sky. Our joy is connected to doing things that make life livable with our own hands. We sawed wood, planted gardens and collected rainwater. When we remove hard work through technology and comfort, we also remove purpose and our ability to say to ourselves, "Look, I did that!"

How many of us dread calling vendors? Calling a company usually sends us into the world of robotic recordings and the seemingly endless struggle to reach a human to answer our questions. After ten minutes of prompts telling us they can understand complete sentences, they always ask if we would like to take a survey at the end of the call. I always say no because it wouldn't matter. For the sake of my blood pressure, I would definitely prefer to reach a human much earlier.

We live in an increasingly artificial world. We live in a world of artificial lighting, with robots who call us more frequently than our friends, and voice recognition software that prevents us from speaking to a real person. It all makes us want to tear our hair out. Machines increasingly gain traction and leave a trail of layoffs in their wake. We now connect to nature through documentaries, not from being out in it. Young people can recognize elephants, but do not know the mammals who live in their backyards.

Just like one of my writing heroes, Richard Louv, I spent my childhood in the woods. This was a time when children were allowed to discover the world on their own. It was a better time and we need to get back to it. I spent my career trying to get kids back into the natural world as an interpretive naturalist. I wrote a book to get inner city kids more comfortable with nature. *Should I Be Afraid* was the title, and I wrote it because I experienced first-hand how children surrounded by cement were afraid of the natural world.

In my thirty-five years of fighting against this world by introducing the beauty of nature, I remember one encounter most vividly. It was from a father who, with tears in his eyes, expressed his gratitude to me for giving his daughter an opportunity "for her feet to touch something other than asphalt and cement." I also recall a woman asking me why the taxidermied ducks on our nature center's shelves weren't moving. She had grown up in a nature-less area of Chicago and had not learned what makes a creature look alive or dead. The stuffed and dusty motionless mounts looked real to her, so her first thought was to wonder how we got them to be so still.

Lack of first-hand knowledge of the natural world creates fear, which is a breeding ground for misinformation. There are endless examples of nonsense I have heard over the years. It would be funny if the crazy ideas didn't often create bad policies.

Mosquitoes, for instance, breed in small puddles of water, pollinate blueberries and feed a whole food chain full of wildlife. They cannot be killed without killing other invertebrates, which then sends a shock wave throughout nature, resulting in the demise of ducks, bats and others who need them for protein. Nature needs mosquitoes to stay in balance. Neighbors of the nature center's marsh often called me asking if I could spray for mosquitoes so that they could have their evening barbeques without disturbance. Since mosquitoes can sometimes spread diseases to humans, a problem easily solved with mosquito netting, we instead use mosquito sprays. Many cities will hire, at great expense, helicopters to spray a listed carcinogen, malathion, to get rid of them.

Fear of nature has also kept us from its true delights. We are so afraid that we might poison ourselves that we refuse to learn the basics about plant identification. I teach that all you need to know to harvest wild plants safely is to know your shapes and colors, and stay away from look -a-likes. Leading hikes about wild edible plants always started with a hike and ended with a dish like Stinging Nettle Fettuccine, much to the amazement of my students. They were further astonished to learn that its nutritional value exceeded store-bought vegetables. Because we are so disconnected from nature and its wonders, many are missing out on one of the best natural highs of life, the discovery of wild edible plants.

We are natural beings. We spent most of our evolutionary history outdoors. It doesn't surprise me that research tells us that we need nature. Researcher Caoimhe Twohig-Bennett from UEA's Norwich Medical School said:

"Spending time in nature certainly makes us feel healthier, but until now the impact on our long-term wellbeing hasn't been fully understood. We gathered evidence from over 140 studies involving more than 290 million people to see whether nature really does provide a health boost. [...] We found that spending time in, or living close to, natural green spaces is associated with diverse and significant health benefits. It reduces the risk of type II diabetes, cardiovascular disease, premature death, and preterm birth, and increases sleep duration."

The health benefits of nature cannot be overstated.

Richard Louv, author of the *Last Child in the Woods*, takes it a step further:

The postmodern notion that reality is only a construct—that we are what we program—suggests limitless human possibilities; but as the young spend less and less of their lives in natural surroundings, their senses narrow, physiologically and psychologically, and this reduces the richness of human experience. … As one scientist puts it, we can now assume that just as children need good nutrition and adequate sleep, they may very well need contact with nature.

Science is also a story. It requires peer reviewed evidence and continual revision under a variety of controlled conditions. Proven facts still battle against well-healed stories rather than evidence.

Science must be reductionist at its core. Yet it is in that very reductionism, something precious is lost. The holistic story of a world that evolved mostly without us has been reduced to a series of parts that capitalism exploits. Anything that turns nature into parts is in danger of selling them to the highest bidder. Until we processed natural gas into propane, we couldn't sell it and it couldn't start its own journey toward scarcity.

In his book *Life Is a Miracle: An Essay against Modern Superstition*, organic farmer, poet and essayist Wendell Berry addresses the assumption, held by many, that science will provide solutions to all the world's problems and mysteries. Berry puts science on the same hot seat that scientists have put religion on for decades. He shines a light on the way science has become its own fallible religion. "To trust 'progress' or our putative "genius" to solve all the problems that we cause is worse than bad science; it is bad religion." Some inventions make perfect sense for most people at the beginning until their full impact is understood. Chlorofluorocarbons (CFCs) were a miracle invention until they were found to dismantle the earth's protective ozone layer. DDTs were intended to save crops from insect plaques, but they killed raptors. Wind turbines are intended to get us off fossil fuels, but they consume a huge amount of resources and kill birds.

The Graduate's character Ben was told "Plastic is the future." Plastic was first synthesized in 1907 by Leo Hendrik Baekeland, a Belgian immigrant to the US. The polymers he created in the lab had many wonderful attributes. They were cheap to make, unbreakable, and long lasting. Plastic is so ubiquitous it is hard to imagine packing a lunch, driving a car, purchasing a smartphone, or doing almost anything without the wonders of light, durable, and cheap plastic. Unfortunately, this invention has been horrible for the same reasons it is wonderful. It takes 450 years, on average, to break down and as the pieces of plastic make their way to the ocean, they have accumulated to the tune of an estimated four-twelve million tons, choking out sunlight needed by coral reefs, and killing sea turtles and seabirds. Those environmental activists on a mission to rid the world of plastic have a fierce battle to fight. The plastic industry is so intertwined in every product sold in the world, from automobiles to shampoo bottles, that it is now a booming four trillion-dollar industry producing an estimated 300 million pounds of plastic per year globally. To stop producing plastic would throw a wrench into the economy as we know it and bring stockbrokers to their knees.

In fact, those invested in the plastics industry are on a warpath to protect their investments. There is an organization called the American Plastic Bag Association. In 2011 they began to lobby for state preemption laws. This means that city councils are prevented from passing local plastics bans. By 2016, forty-two percent of Americans could not legally pass local bans on plastics. None of this is because plastic is good for us. It is because it is good for business. When our narrative favors business over the health of the Earth, all species lose. The oceans lose, the turtles lose, the corals lose, and temporarily the rich get filthy rich.

The jobs associated with plastic and other synthetic production have played a role in the great disconnection from nature. Many people lucky enough to earn a living wage, spend the majority of their waking hours inside with artificial lighting, recycled air and lack of windows. Specialization of labor has taken us even further away from the natural world. Not only do others produce our goods, they grow our food products in ways that have also been industrialized. Today's farmers mostly work for large corporately owned farms and plant our corn and soybeans from inside their air-conditioned combines.

People need to be taught how to enjoy nature's beauty and learn from experiences in nature. For the first two decades of my career as a naturalist, I could count on the excitement of my students about going out on the trails. I remember the day at my nature center when high school students from an urban environment felt fearful of going where things could "get them." It taught me how quickly we can lose our natural connection to the outdoors. Isolation in urban environments has taken a terrible toll and even instigated a fear of the natural world. Technology has also disconnected us from nature. It is very difficult to make good choices when we are more familiar with the synthetic world than we are the natural one.

The isolation and quarantine in our enclosed environments brought on by the Coronavirus pandemic has confirmed that we are not meant to live isolated from the outside world. People are going crazy cooped up with only their devices to guide them through the maze of survival. If it were natural to stay inside, we would be doing much better. It is not just the lack of freedom we rebel against, but the need to feel the sun on our faces and the wind in our hair while looking at the sky with its endless designs of clouds passing by.

The natural world, when we can connect to it, can give us much needed solace and perspective. Without an ability to go to the gym for exercise, people find places to safely walk and seek out the beauty of nature. Nature was always there, but it is now just what the doctor ordered. Discovering that there is beauty and calm in these outdoor parks and natural areas is at least a small dividend of this awful, life-crushing virus.

We are also discovering in our overpopulated world how quickly parks can get overrun with too many visitors. Those unaccustomed to being in nature are now there and, combined with the reduction in park employees, huge litter problems have developed. We have to re-teach people how to respectfully be outdoors and how too much human visitation often spells trouble for the solace we seek. We are trying to socially distance ourselves and then discover that the parade of our fellow citizens trying to do the same is ruining the experience. It's a harsh lesson to finally discover the benefits of nature at time when our cities are packed with people clamoring to get out.

Chapter 5

From the Other to Us

Auschwitz was bu lt not with stones, but words.

—Rabbi Abraham Heschel

As the philosopher and writer Eckhart Tolle said, "To love is to recognize yourself in another."

We can't settle for a world where our numbers perfectly align with our resources; we must also focus on the quality of our lives. It has become clear in recent days that white supremacists are alive and well all over the country and the world. We must recognize the dark side of our human character and irradiate it at every opportunity. We need to become better humans who see the humanity in all of us. Our actions can restore our pride in how we treat each other and take responsibility for systems, laws and individuals who feed old narratives of inequality.

I wrote the first draft of this chapter months before the filmed murder of George Floyd, a Black man, at the hands of a white Minneapolis police officer. The world has since exploded. My hometown is now infamous for being one more place where common brutality rocks a community unable to break free of a horrid narrative. What will it take to see real change? When will justice arrive? We are at a historic moment where a new narrative could be taking shape. Enough people from around the globe say that they will not stop speaking out until Black lives matter. They are joining hands en masse during the COVID-19 pandemic in a force of unprecedented solidarity. From New Zealand to England, from New York to San Francisco, people are demanding that not only should violent police be prosecuted, but that this fear, brutality, murder and injustice needs to stop happening. They are demanding that we start valuing the lives of the oppressed. Let's hope we are bearing witness to the death of our deeply embedded, immoral racist narrative.

Together we must seek a better public and private discourse in this country and around the world, one based on a compassionate understanding of who we need to and can be. We have long been swimming in a sea of classism, racism, and xenophobia that is growing more toxic by the day. But we are not all like that. We are capable of so much more, yet this is a very difficult journey because we are tied to the stories of our time and place.

Many of us shun hatred as a framework for living. This means the dominant narrative can change. It has to. In the 2015 film *A Rising Tide*, the lead character described that what we cook has to go beyond being good enough. It must be as good as it can be. That struck a chord with me. It is not good enough to tolerate each other. We must be as good as we can be and embrace the other within ourselves. We don't have to agree; in fact, we can emphatically disagree, but we must never dismiss or undervalue the humanity in each person no matter what their perceived differences. Indeed, we are the only species haunted by our own mortality and struggle to come to terms with it in a variety of ways. We worry about our loved ones, and our ability to support them. Beyond those species- specific similarities, each culture, race and gender group has deeply different histories. The Dalai Lama once wrote, "Love and compassion are necessities, not luxuries. Without them humanity cannot survive." But it is difficult to walk down that road when it has been paved with lies. When the door to the painful truth of oppression has been surgically and strategically removed from our history books and thus from our cultural narrative, we have little hope that the sea change we need will ever happen. We must know the brutal truth about each other's history, to begin the healing we need so desperately. Books like *Lies My Teacher Told Me, Everything Your American History Textbook Got Wrong*, by James W. Loewen, and *The People's History of the United States* by Howard Zinn need to become standard high school textbooks among others. We cannot keep erasing history because we do not want to come to grips with its implications.

What we have done to one another in the name of power, greed, hatred and fear could fill libraries, yet few Americans know about the events that would illuminate our shame if told in their grisly details. The way the Tulsa-Greenwood massacre, the murderous killing and burning of blacks and their businesses in 1921, was covered up is but one example of the history we are not taught. How many know what the museum of National Peace and Justice stands for or that we even have one? It is imperative that we know the real history of slavery, who participated and who benefited. We need to know that what followed it included the terror of lynching which causes six million blacks to flee to the north.

The PBS series "Finding Your Roots with Henry Louis Gates, Jr.," revisits American history through the lens of those who suffered its wrath. On an episode focused on slavery, they found that Jesuit priests who escaped Europe in order to be free to practice their religion became not only slave owners, but slave traders when tobacco was the crop of the day. Men of the cloth demanded their own freedom but could easily enslave others because they did not see them as equals. Freedom cannot only be valued for those who look like us and believe like we do, yet this narrative is repeated so often one could mine the stories for several doctoral thesis projects.

Not only is our shameful past often shoved into the back pages of history, but the achievements of non-dominant groups are also swept aside so that they can remain undervalued in a world that prefers one group, white protestant males dominate and have access to the most privilege. The Tuskegee Airmen, a black military group, that flew over 15,000 missions over Europe during world war II but were not officially recognized for their bravery until 2007. History books are void of the accomplishments of all but a few women who were responsible for great achievements. There is a reason, for example, we don't hear much about Jeannette Rankin. To acknowledge that she was the first congresswoman elected to the United States congress or that she served two terms or lobbied for woman's suffrage would give women too much power, and open the way for their empowerment. Struggles of non-dominant racial and gender groups have a long and painful past which continues shamefully into the present. All of these stories need to told, preferably in their own voices. Bigotry is the wedge that keeps us from changing narrative. It is based on convenient lies that keep the power structure in place. Bulldozing its existence starts with telling the truth from the perspective of the powerless.

Seeing women and children as inferior and therefore exploitable, reveals a deep state of otherness.

Modern slavery is, unfortunately, alive and well in the world today. Defined in different terms, it is ingrained in so many evil narratives. According to the International Labour Organization:

An estimated 40.3 million men, women, and children were victims of modern slavery on any given day in 2016. Of these, 24.9 million people were in forced labor and 15.4 million people were living in a forced marriage. Women and girls are vastly over-represented, making up 71 percent of victims. ... The current Global Estimates do not cover all forms of modern slavery; for example, organ trafficking, child soldiers, or child marriage that could also constitute forced marriage are not able to be adequately measured at this time. Arab States are affected by substantial gaps in the available data. Given this is a region that hosts 17.6 million migrant workers, representing more than one-tenth of all migrant workers in the world and one in three workers in the Arab States, and one in which forced marriage is reportedly widespread, the current estimate is undoubtedly a significant underestimate.

Unfortunately, we cannot look to the past for guidance. War has been with us forever, even in pre-colonial America. In his book *Lakota America*, Pekka Hämäläinen describes in great detail the kinship between certain tribes and the wars between others. Kin were protected while enemies were enslaved or killed. Alliances between tribes didn't happen until it was necessary to fight the colonization by Europeans and their superior weapons of war and disease.

In our globalized world with too many nuclear warheads, tanks, missiles, and bombs to count, we are deeply threatened by hanging on to narratives that support war. Not only is war costly in lives, but it is costly in fossil fuel and resources. Not only does war cost us morally, but it has a huge environmental impact. The United States army uses more fossil fuel than any other sovereign nation, and that's not even when we are at war.

Genocides have been perpetrated on ethnic minorities throughout history, and to this day, because a dangerous story captivated the majority or those in power. Propaganda is both an old and modern-day pathway that encourages the destruction of people falsely deemed evil. If enough people act, and enough look away, evil is given a permission slip.

Richter, Marks and Tait published their findings in *Public Health Review* on October 22, 2018. They articulated the steps needed in order for genocide to happen:

- Dehumanization: Dehumanization is used by perpetrators to evoke feelings of loathing, contempt, and revulsion, often by comparing or identifying the target with nonhuman species or diseases.

- Demonization: Blaming the target for the perpetrators' personal misfortunes or those of his/her group and/or provoking feelings of fear towards a specific group.
- Delegitimization: Denying the existence or history of the other group, and/or accusing the target of extreme criminal acts.
- Disinformation: Presenting false or partial information with the intent to malign.
- Denial: Negating historical facts or denying past atrocities.
- Threats: Statements of intent to inflict pain, injury, damage, or other hostile action on groups or individuals.
- Glorification of terror: Invoking well-known perpetrators of genocidal violence as role models (such as the memorializing "martyrs" or financial compensation for families of "martyrs" or terrorists

The beginning of it all starts with dehumanization. Dehumanization could not happen without the support of organized religion, classism, and racism. They are all foundations for viewing those with different pedigrees as less than equal. Differences on a planet of seven continents, distributed over many ecosystems and political boundaries, are not only expected but they make life so interesting. It is wonderful to have different languages, music, cuisine, dance, and art, but differences of class, race, and religion must not be grounds for mistreatment, hatred, and murder. Simmering under the surface of most cultures are the beliefs that some groups are inherently inferior. Jews have the burden of carrying anti-Semitism's toxic stories with them into every corner of the world, and when society feels threatened by economic downturns and nationalistic fevers, they are often the first to be scapegoated for society's woes.

Many religions still teach that a person born disabled is a curse from god, which is another reason that worship must be converted to wonder. In India, for instance, the disabled are shunned and put into inhumane institutions. In 2020 Michelle and Barack Obama produced *Crip Camp*, a documentary film about the historic fight for the rights of the disabled in the US. It took hunger strikes and years of coordinated efforts from disabled activists to just get the right to have access to buildings and bathroom stalls. We now take the American Disabilities Act for granted. We expect everything from buses to playgrounds to be accessible, but that was a battle that shouldn't have taken so long. It was not signed into law until 1990 under President George H.W. Bush. While some argued that the cost of making everything accessible seemed prohibitive, the stigma against those with disabilities had a long sordid history. If we changed our narrative to one that appreciated the other in us, it wouldn't be so challenging for justice for all abilities to rule the land.

I have been fortunate to be able-bodied most of my life. Years ago, I was stricken with a rare disease that caused me to lose the ability to walk for several months. I discovered that the phrase, 'We are all just temporarily able bodied,' is true. It gave me an even greater compassion for those who cannot easily move through life. We must remove all stigmas and treat others like we want to be treated, especially those with disabilities. The golden rule, of treating everyone as we wish to be treated, applies to all and that must dominate our country and our world.

Socrates said, "The unexamined life is not worth living," and the unexamined narratives that determine how we treat each other are not worth keeping. These narratives are all related. When we favor capitalism, we promote classism and the degradation of the planet's resources. When we give power to religion, we create the concept of the other, or one who is not us. So when "those" people are given poor wages or enslaved, it is conveniently justified because they are not us.

While social justice and peace are the goal, they are not possible in a world of scarcity. War is driven mainly by the need and greed for resources in a growing world. A bumper sticker during one of the last Middle East wars had these words of wisdom: "How did our oil get under their sand?" Domination of others is also driven by the belief that one's economic narrative or religious beliefs are superior and should become the dominant narrative for everyone. Scarcity is driven by overpopulation and greed. Too much concentration of wealth at the top robs the multitudes of a decent life. No one owns golden bathroom fixtures and multiple mansions without creating suffering.

When we see the reasons why the world is in the dire shape it is, we will no longer keep looking at just one flaw in our world. The perfect storm made up of our mistrust of each other, our unexamined belief systems, our unchallenged economic systems, our greedy actions, and our lack of ecological fitness is fueling the multiple problems we are facing and will continue to face until we rip off the bandages and address the wounds underneath.

Seeing the other as us needs to be taken even deeper. We need to see ourselves as a part of the web of life. We depend on the natural world. It does not need us and would be so much better off without us.

Every two years, World Wildlife Fund releases their "The Living Planet Report." In 2018 it reported that mammals, birds, fish and amphibians have shrunk by sixty percent in just forty years. We are not sharing the planet well. It remains frustrating every time that NGOs like World Wildlife Fund cannot type the word "overpopulation" and instead use the euphemism "human activity" to explain away this horrid phenomenon. So not only do we refuse to admit non-human species into our story, but we will not even take the full responsibility for doing so.

Mainstream news headlines never lead with a lost species. The only way to find orangutans hanging on for dear life from the last remaining trees in Borneo is on nature shows. News stories are full of human-based narratives. Accidents, explosions, strikes, diseases, taxes, and tomorrow's weather are all focused on our well-being, but not really. It is a delusion that we are separate from our wildlife or domestic animal cousins, to their peril and ours. They are the most disenfranchised "other" as they do not have a way to petition their way onto the stage of inclusion.

As noted by Gary Snyder, author of "The Practice of the Wild": "The extinction of species, each one a pilgrim of four billion years of evolution, is an irreversible loss. The ending of the lines of so many creatures with whom we have traveled this far is an occasion of profound sorrow and grief. Death can be accepted and to some degree transformed. But the loss of lineages and all their future young is not something to accept. It must be rigorously and intelligently resisted.

Those who have taken on the issue of illuminating the cruelty of factory farming have made some progress in challenging our narrative that animals do not suffer, but they are still the minority. In spite of Dr. Jane Goodall's work, among others, on the sentient nature of other species, the narrative of our superiority continues to be in charge. Fighting those who hate to see the beaks cut off live chickens, or calves isolated in darkness ripped away from their mothers to produce veal, is agri-business, with billions of dollars in advertising about the scrumptious and cheap availability of deep fried and battered meat awaiting your next visit to a drive through window. What goes unsaid behind the finger-lickin good story, is that you are eating suffering and gobbling up resources faster than the Earth can replace them.

With compassion as our lens, I believe we do have it within us to begin to incorporate other cultures, ethnicities, races and even other species into our worldview. If we don't want to keep sliding ever more rapidly towards the cliff of both moral and physical collapse, we have to do things differently. Radical change is required; even though the evidence that we are capable of that change is flimsy.

Many who study our ecological decline, would say that humankind will run its course and go extinct like the dinosaurs. We are arguably, our own meteor, the top predator of our time. That catastrophic event some sixty-five million years ago, created a new niche for primates. Our departure will open the door for the next predator to rule the Earth. Someday another creature will evolve to take our place high on the food chain sometime before our yellow star comes to the end of its life a few billion years from now.

But what if we collectively realized, at a deep level, that we are on a high-speed extinction train dragging so many other species with us? I believe, naively perhaps, that we should try to stop the train knowing that there will be so many innocent victims of our unwillingness to change. After all, we are the species who traveled to the moon, painted the Mona Lisa and produced the great music of our lives.

Chapter 6

From Mindless
to Mindful

Fight for the things that you believe in but do it
in a way that will lead others to join you

—Ruth Bader Ginsburg

Buddhist philosopher and meditation teacher Thich Nhat Hanh said in December 2019, "When your mindfulness becomes powerful, your concentration becomes powerful, and when you are fully concentrated, you have a chance to make a breakthrough, to achieve insight." We desperately need insight, especially when our so-called leaders are leading us into the abyss. We must also live higher on the time and space continuum. We are the only species with an ability to see into the future and we must find the courage to become more mindful in a world where growth economics wants us to remain asleep.

More research needs to be done on this topic, but in a 2017 paper, "Mindfulness in Sustainability Science Practice and Healing," Wamsler et al concluded: "Mindfulness can contribute to understanding and facilitating sustainability, not only at the individual level, but sustainability at all scales, and should, thus, become a core concept in sustainability science, practice, and teaching."

But in the world today, companies take advantage of our mindlessness and saturate us with endless commercials. Billions are spent each year convincing us of a problem we did not know we had so that we can solve it with a product we did not know we needed. There are entire networks devoted strictly to shopping for products we think we need to make our lives easier, when they are only designed to make a few individuals very rich. The rest of us end up getting rid of these so-called miracle products in garage sales or landfills years later.

Weight Watchers and other diet groups teach that we must stop mindless eating. While we watch TV and shove food into our mouths, we are unaware of the calories we are consuming and, as a result, we gain weight. Yoga instructors teach us to pay attention to our breath and the way our body feels in order to address stress. We need to heed this advice and become more mindful of what we are doing to each other, to other species, and to the planet. So much of what we do goes unquestioned. Those who dare to question often get into trouble. We need a revolution of thought, attitude, and principles. Resistance is hard but acceptance has consequences not too far down the road.

As a naturalist, I am fascinated with the natural history of all species. I loved learning, for instance, that there is a caterpillar in Romania that can mimic the scent of ants and, once captured, can trick them into caring for its life. I am intrigued by the adaptations of so many creatures. In all of my studies, however, I have never found evidence that other life forms record history and can conceptualize what the future might be like based on current practices. Even though we are capable of more, there is a reason the philosopher George Santayana once said, "Those who cannot remember the past are condemned to repeat it."

Policies are set in boardrooms and in the halls of Congress, both state and local. The average citizen is given narrow choices. We get to choose between the organic apples wrapped in plastic and the pesticide-laden ones in "better" packaging. We get to choose the energy efficient appliances, but only if we have the money to spend.

It goes deeper than this. Our economic system is based on today's Wall Street numbers and the fiscal year. There's not much opportunity to think into the future when your job and portfolio are riding on high stakes that see the future as a luxury.

Changing from a philosophy of what feels good today to what will feel good tomorrow is critical to our future. Richard Fisher, managing editor of the BBC, wrote on January 9, 2019:

> Part of the problem is that the "now" commands so much more attention. We are saturated with knowledge and standards of living have mostly never been higher—but today it is difficult to look beyond the next news cycle. The 24/7 news cycle can usually handle only one big news story at a time. It has us conditioned to respond to only the most awful things happening now. Many things can and should be prevented by paying at-

tention to life's everyday problems. Noticing that improvements on highways never yield less traffic, for instance, could lead to challenging road-widening as a response to growing demand for space on our roadways. If time can be sliced, it is only getting finer, with ever-shorter periods now shaping our world.

To paraphrase the investor Esther Dyson: "In politics the dominant time frame is a term of office, in fashion and culture it's a season. For corporations it's a quarter, on the internet it's minutes, and on the financial markets mere milliseconds." Capitalism redefines the timeframe through which we make decisions. Destroying a river in order to save money on cleanup is not a problem when the fiscal year is elevated over the significance of what that means for the future of clean water.

It is hard to be mindful, however, when one is trying to survive at the most basic level of life. A man in Laos who just had to kill the pygmy slow loris for dinner is not going to spend much time pondering the future of the animal's existence. In these cases, the level of consciousness that must protect wildlife needs to happen at the policy level. For years it was a competition to see who could catch the largest catfish in the Mekong River. This species weighed up to 650 pounds and due to overfishing from a growing population, ninety percent have disappeared. Now it is illegal to catch them. Mindfulness at the state level often kicks in too late.

Being mindful is a way to do a gut check with the information you hear. It's a way to slow down and see how we are doing and how we might do better. Modern living often has us running around so fast we barely notice each other, especially now that it is forecasted that the average person will be spending fifteen years of their more diminished life on their smartphones. Something drastic has to happen for us to take notice. We are conditioned to pay attention to life's biggest woes.

We have a gift. Libraries, and now the Internet, are full of information and examples of humanity's successes and failures. We are a species that can learn and apply what we learn to changing our course. What researching this book has taught me, however, is that when we are invested emotionally and economically in a way of doing things, change becomes difficult. It gets more challenging when ideas are attributed to doctrines of faith.

Today when we hear the words "Seventh Generation," we may think of green cleaning products, or toilet paper that is being hoarded. But the idea is ancient and powerful. As Faithkeeper of the Onondaga

Nation Oren Lyons (Seneca) once said, "The Peacemaker taught us about the Seven Generations. He said, when you sit in council for the welfare of the people, you must not think of yourself or of your family, not even of your generation. He said, make your decisions on behalf of the seven generations coming, so that they may enjoy what you have today." Wise advice much needed in our world of mindless consumption today. We need to stop and get off the merry go round long enough to see what is happening. To see the errors of our ways is just a first step but a critical one.

Mindfulness would be easier if solitude was considered to be an inalienable right, included in our values of life, liberty and the pursuit of happiness. Solitude requires open space away from the trappings and noise of the modern human environment. Solitude allows for thoughts and feelings to be pondered at a deeper level. As our society becomes drenched in more people, more development, more devices and greater despair, solitude and its possibilities for mindfulness slips away.

Yoga, qi (chi) gong and other naturopathic practitioners encourage us to breathe deeply and move in ways that push aside the demands of the modern world and seek an inner peace. These practices are even used in some innovative classrooms to get students to focus on their studies and on treating each other with more respect. Now that the COVID pandemic has relegated our learning environments to be more at home, these tools to achieve mindfulness could and should be implemented to give children the tools that they will need to process what is happening in the world around them.

Chapter 7

Weaving it All Together

We delight in the beauty of the butterfly, but
rarely admit the changes it has gone through to
achieve that beauty.

—Maya Angelou

The task to change these deeply ingrained stories can feel like trying
to climb Mount Everest, barefoot and backwards. Many will say we
cannot change, and they have a lot of evidence on their side. But that
does not mean we should not try our best to make those changes,
especially when so much is at stake. I find much strength when I look
to the early abolitionists. Back in 1850, there were over three million
slaves held on over 46,000 plantations in the southern states of the
US. It was a deeply ingrained way of life held together by many false,
oppressive narratives, punishments and horrific conditions. Yet for
decades, black and white abolitionists risked their lives to fight against
the tyranny of slavery. They didn't buckle under the unlikelihood of
success. Neither should we.

The barriers to changing narratives are not unlike the Kubler-
Ross model of grief. We don't want to change because we do not want
to accept a difficult truth or, in this case, many difficult truths. It is
comfortable to stay with what we know, and we are understandably
afraid of what is ahead. The biggest barrier to change is the first stage:
denial. So many are in denial of what I have laid out in this book
that they will move quickly to being angry at me for suggesting these
radical changes. People respond best to narrative, not straight
information. They must hear a new story that they
accept, and those of us who live and breathe science

have to get better at storytelling and gluing those stories together with songs, dance and other art forms.

We are hard-wired to respond to narrative, mostly oral narrative. Baked into the human DNA is a prescription for listening to oral histories, not absorbing scientific data. Humans, in our current form, have been on Earth for approximately 200,000 years. Of those years 189,000 or so were spent as hunter-gatherers. During all that time, we relied on elders to pass on vital information about how to grow and hunt for food and survive in a world that had not yet been converted to a human playground. They did this with pictures they could draw with burnt wooden sticks, stone engravings and stories told around fires, reinforced with dances and celebrations. We did not question our elders because they were the keepers of the story and there was no alternative. We need to figure out a way to change our stories by telling better ones.

The six narratives illustrated here are deeply linked. As Greta Thunberg, our young heroic climate activist from Sweden, has said, "After all, the climate crisis is not just about the environment. It is a crisis of human rights, of justice and of political will. Colonial, racist and patriarchal systems of oppression have created and fueled it. We need to dismantle them all. Our political leaders can no longer shirk their responsibilities." Indeed, the existential threat of our climate crisis is a symptom of what I call the "disease of thought." We think we can overcome our limits with technology. We think we can continue to go on as we are, and if some genius will figure out cold fusion and all will be right with the world.

I disagree with the semantics of the collapse warnings I see in the prevailing literature. It is not that I challenge that collapse is where we are headed; it is that collapse should be avoided. We don't want our tent to collapse when it is up, we don't want our friendships to collapse because we want and need them. We need to stop wanting the world we have created and want something else. We say we want to end homelessness, promote wildlife, and end traffic congestion. But do we really? Are we willing to examine how we actually got here and change course?

To me, to fear collapse of the status quo is to be unaware that it is not what we need or want. The narratives that I have articulated in this book are not serving us. They are not sustainable. They create a world which will indeed collapse, and the world of those narratives should collapse. I would prefer that we choose new ways of living on this earth and leave the old ones behind, but we are deeply invested in them and the pain of extrication is great. I would rather see language built around negating our old ways instead of worrying that they are ending. I was asked recently in an interview if I was a "doomer." That term referred to someone resigned to the idea that we are witnessing the end of the world as we know it. I told him that I do not identify with that term. Intellectually I cannot disagree with the grim place we find ourselves in, but emotionally I cannot live there. I want the world of inequity and of worshipping false gods to end. I think there is efficacy in trying to articulate those possibilities. Let us celebrate, not mourn, what must end. I want to readjust so that sandhill cranes can continue to fly and clouded leopards can go on roaming this earth. Deep change is to be celebrated. I would like our energies to go into creating the kind of world we can continue to live in and have the courage to let the others go. Once I realized what agri-business was doing to the land and atmosphere, it didn't take me long to stop eating their products. Few followed my example because there is so much money behind promoting the current paradigm. Few alternatives are offered.

There are countless class action lawsuits by plaintiffs claiming deception by companies, ranging from using known carcinogens in their products to making false health claims. This is all a result of the way neo-capitalism, or growth economics, rules our world. Government regulation should be in place to protect the public, but without solid campaign finance reform, regulations are continually weakened because politicians are funded by self-serving corporations. Why do products go on the market without rigorous testing? Why do we have to prove something is toxic to our world after it has already done damage? They should have to prove it is safe. That would be far more likely to happen in a world built on stories more respectful to our earth, less attached to the Ponzi scheme of growth and less dismissive of the laws of physics.

I was asked to write for a blog site called Jewcology.org. I published the following on September 5, 2019, referring to how we need to take our narratives and expand them to include a broader truth:

> Tikkun Olam is a deeply Jewish ethic that is supposed to be about valuing the repairing of the world. It too becomes a euphemism when it does not include the recognition of the oppressive nature of overpopulation. To repair our world, we must open our eyes and hearts to the cold-hard facts about how rapidly we are going in the opposite direction from Tikkun Olam.

In the time it has taken me to write this, 10,000 new passengers have been added net gain to Mother Earth, and She now needs to find dwindling resources to support them.

Once we deeply understand the fallout from our growing human populations and the way that we deplete the very resources we need because we cannot help but consume as apex predators, we will find solutions. Smoking isn't just dangerous, smoking kills us. We now have laws in place that have started working because we know the true nature of the problem. We must start the journey towards true Tikkun Olam. We need to do so without euphemistically painting a picture that excludes our frighteningly high human numbers. I hope it's not too late.

Indeed, each religion has a hook from which we can crack open a door to a more holistic look at life and our future on Earth. Knowing that religion is often the gatekeeper to change, years ago I became active in a group called the Minnesota Interfaith Ecology Coalition. Prior to Earth Day, we sent mailings to clergy, and changed the contents of the envelope depending on the particular religious group. I recall with great clarity the laughter I broke into when both the significance and the silliness of this effort hit me. Each group needed its own reason for saving the planet when we all live here. We looked for an appropriate biblical quote to get the pastors, priests and rabbis to pay attention and do something significant for Earth Day. Some were more receptive than others. It turns out, however, that deep change was never on their agenda. They were willing to change their light bulbs and sources of energy but went nowhere near issues like overpopulation and the human takeover of the planet.

Readers can guess what I think the chances are that any of these narratives will be flipped. It is hard to see how any one of the old stories will be abandoned in time. They all need to be left in the dust. I must be clear that the change we need is radical. I liken it to looking at Mt. Rushmore and the patriotic narrative it represents and see it instead through the eyes of the many Native American tribes who refer to it as the Paha Sapa. The Paha Sapa, according to their narrative, is a place where their gods and ancestors live. It is holy ground. Carving up those mountains into images of the white man's leaders is a blasphemy to them. I recall attending a ceremony at Mt. Rushmore, complete with red, white and blue lights and patriotic music. I wondered then how it might feel if you were from a First Nation people witnessing that celebration at your sacred site. Seeing the world through different eyes is the beginning.

One encouraging story is the story of CFCs mentioned earlier. Once the word got out that CFCs were destroying the ozone layer, people and companies abandoned them before they were officially banned. Let's hope this example is illustrative of our potential. Apparently, we can change before we are forced to because it is life-saving. Cynics might say that there wasn't much sacrifice involved in the case of CFCs, but at least we know we can be redirected. United States automakers were forced by law to have higher mileage standards. Customers got used to the idea. When the laws were removed by those in bed with the oil companies, the consumer demand kept the standards in place. That is one way we can buck the system.

I have experienced a radical change of story in my lifetime. In my 30s, I belonged to a health club in Minnesota that had a smoking section. I remember when the full story of secondhand smoke was not understood. We had airplanes allowing smoking in the back of their vessels. Relentless pressure from health professionals, investigative reporters, legislators and the families of those who suffered the loss of those killed by the diseases it perpetrated helped to change the laws. In 2008, the Clean Indoor Air Act was passed followed by policies dictating that smoking cannot even occur outdoors. Only after society had a shift of stories was I able to ban smoking at the nature center I directed. In the early '90s when I started running the park, smoking and the subsequent litter was a daily annoyance. But the protests would have been loud and difficult had I not waited until the story had shifted to change the rules. Not until it was understood that cigarette smoking and secondary smoke was a public health hazard could I decree that smoking could only be done inside one's car in the parking lot. Upon enforcing the law, I got only apologies, not protests, because it was collectively understood that the story had changed. It went from being a personal freedom to being a public health concern. The rules followed without need for much enforcement and were very easy to put into place.

The old story of coal mining is still with us. Prior to his election, President Trump campaigned in mining country. He promised to bring their coal mining jobs back. His ridiculous statements were received with roaring applause. Even though burning coal is the single biggest contributor to climate change, even though these jobs guarantee a short life span and horrid working conditions to workers, the narrative was entrenched. Coal mining began just after 1800. Lifestyles in Appalachia were built around it and the industrial revolution depended on it. Scientists can scream about it, activists can protest, but a presidential candidate saying pandering things about an old story can overcome all of the evidence; that is, unless someone comes around and tells a better story. Innovating new rural cottage industries with investments in training a workforce has a ring to it that enough people might respond to if it is told and sold well.

Using smoking's history as an example, we need hard evidence and buy-in by many. We need messaging to be concise and widespread. I do recall an effective bus poster showing rats that had been killed by poison. The caption read "The same poison that killed these rats is in cigarettes." We need to jar people awake while also supporting a new way of being in the world.

The Coronavirus also invites us to make radical change. We will see what shakes out.

I have no delusions that my book, or any other book, can be enough of a catalyst to change the world. This is an anonymous quote from the School of Life website:

> A book is of course an ideal place to lay down an ambition, sort out one's thoughts and gather a constituency. But that's about it. A book on its own cannot bring about real change because the world as it currently stands isn't held together simply by ideas: it is made up of laws, practices, institutions, financial arrangements, businesses and governments. In other words, its muscles are made up of institutions and therefore, the only way to bring about real change is to act through competing institutions. Revolutions in consciousness cannot be made lasting and effective until legions of people start to work together in concert for a common aim and, rather than relying on the intermittent pronouncements of mountain-top prophets, begin the unglamorous and deeply boring task of wrestling with issues of law, money, long-term mass communication, advocacy and administration...

The world isn't being changed as effectively as it should be, largely because most of us are forgetting to study the lessons that can be drawn from religion. We should use the history of religion to inform us about the role of repetition, ritual, and beauty in the name of changing how things are. Repetition, ritual, and beauty can and need to be employed to change our narratives.

In ancient China the philosopher Confucius transformed his war-torn country by offering a new way of thinking about the world. Born 551 years before the common era, his ideas offer much to our modern problems. In a concept he called "Junzi," he proposed that rituals be created around the concept of creating a more noble and moral character in each of us regardless of one's station in life. He created a moral code and then rituals to accompany them. I believe his ideas offer a great structural opportunity to reimagine our world.

We love tradition, and ritual helps us to stay on track. But we need it to coalesce around more relevant messages, ones that proclaim a space for a less greedy, limited, unified and worship free world.

The deepest of ironies is that we both promote humans and treat them with disdain. We favor humans when we plow up the Earth for their housing and we hurt them when we do not and cannot provide for their needs.

How do we live in a world when we both need more human rights and fewer humans? We embrace conflicting stories often without realizing it. In the murkiness of what it means to be human in this century is a simultaneous need to be more humane and less arrogant in promoting of our species over others.

Readers should be asking, "So, what do we do?"

It's overwhelming, isn't it? Just remember that story MUST come before solutions. Imagine showing up for a required surgical procedure and not knowing why. We would not show up. To get us to keep our appointment, we need to know that we need it and we can recover. I now spend many days not seeing one smoker. Only decades ago, non-smokers could not listen to music in bars without being engulfed in carcinogenic vapor. Smoking wasn't easily banned because we not only thought smoking was cool, but it was promoted as a lifestyle by major corporations. Examine how smoking flipped and follow that pattern.

While our government was violating treaties, pushing native peoples off their lands, and sending their children to abusive boarding schools, what was the dominant story? This battle still rages, and the story has not changed all that much. We still don't respect the rights or knowledge of those who inhabited the lands of the now United States before dominant culture began the slaughter. Tribal nations who are fighting to stop pipelines, mining and the theft of water and land don't just do it as a tug of war; they do it to protect their way of life and Mother Earth, which many now recognize as a better path. I saw many tribal people dressed in their traditional clothing at the 2019 UN Climate Change Conference COP 25 in Spain. I was in awe of their determination to tell their story of how their destruction meant the earth's destruction. Recent victories to stop rainforest destruction and the way they tell their story are a blueprint for our effort to change ours. In 2019, the Waorani people of Ecuador successfully defended half a million acres of Indigenous territory in the Amazon rainforest from oil drilling. They were relentless and attached the drilling as a direct hit to their way of life. Their fight is surely not over, but it was a victory of their story over the dominant toxic one. Changing narrative often starts with class action lawsuits preceded by tragedy and followed by awareness; still, change is hard when investors back the corporate path, buy out the politicians and fund the ads to support their greed.

Struggles aren't going to get easier, but we must have the right target in mind. We first must ask why we got here and what is underneath it all. We just may need to create a violence-free genre of films, an antidote to the current positive reception enjoyed by violence, so that reasonable gun legislation can finally be implemented. Yes, we need to offer legislative solutions, but more importantly we have to degrade gun culture. We have to put the effort into decoupling the ties that bind us to dangerous narratives. The truth is often the opposite of what we believe, but in order to change that we have to give people something else to believe.

Life is like crossing a river. It is dangerous, but we do our best to move from rock to rock and make our way across without falling in. Changing stories is about offering people better rocks to walk on. The great minds of our world offered new rocks; they did not just tell us to stop crossing the river.

There is encouraging news coming out of the world of mycology. Fungus is being successfully used to clean up toxic oil spill sites. Understanding how mushrooms work to support trees is helping to plant a green belt to stop desertification in Africa. Imagine how much better our world would be if restoration was our dominant narrative. Controlling the narrative is our greatest challenge because the competition is false narratives told by those invested in keeping things from going off the cliff. The challenge is alarming in its magnitude.

As an educator and naturalist, I have learned that I cannot control outcomes; I can just control my voice and what I say about our predicament as we begin a new decade of life on this planet. The good news is that humans who live in relatively free societies are often very creative storytellers. Theatrically gifted people thrill audiences with stories on screen and stage. Authors weave tales and get on the bestseller lists. Our artists know how to tell new stories. We need to encourage their creativity at every opportunity. We can teach how bad stories must die and be replaced by ones that weave a web of justice and true sustainability. This book is my effort to give readers a flashlight so that we can find our way into the light and hopefully provide compelling encouragement to begin that difficult but necessary discussion.

Let me simplify a very complex concept into four things, a very arrogant but perhaps a necessary thing to do:

1) We have to discard our love affair with rote learning and testing our students ad nauseum. We are preparing automatons for boring jobs, not the leaders and responsible citizens we need. We have to embrace a new way of educating young and old alike. Critical thinking must be at the heart of the way we teach in this country and around the world. As educator and teacher trainer Brian Oshiro so brilliantly put it, "If we want our children to have flexible minds that can readily absorb new information and respond to complex problems, we need to develop their critical thinking skills." Assistant Ideas Editor at TED, Mary Halton, used Oshiro's examples and pointed to the way we must go in her April 2019 article, part of TED's "How to Be a Better Human" series. Educators need to use the whole article as a roadmap for the four things critical thinking must incorporate: 1) Go beyond "what?" — and ask "how?" and "why?," localizing knowledge with examples when possible; 2) Ask "How do you know this?" , 3) Prompt them to think about how their perspective may differ from other people's 4) Finally, ask them how to solve this problem.

2) We must take every opportunity to rebuke the notion that humans can overtake the planet without creating our own death march. We need to develop our compassion for all species and the way we are all a part of the same cosmic dust. Growth economics deserves our collective hatred for its devastating effects on our planet's resources. Let's embrace ecological economics, which puts the Earth before money and respects the laws of physics, knowing that economic systems are always a subset of our earth.

3) We need to employ a more positive approach to changing our narratives. Threats only inspire people to retreat. Start to paint a picture of the positive things that can happen if we successfully change. Alon Tal and Dorit Kerret discussed using positive psychology in a paper called, "Positive psychology as a strategy for promoting sustainable population policies." They describe the benefits of focusing our attention on the world that will get better from change. When we explain the benefits of changing our ways, we will get more results than shouting about the doom ahead.

4) Most importantly, we have to become the loudest voice in the room by telling more scientifically supported stories that are also supported by dances, songs, and art that reinforces and repeats truly sustainable stories.

For my sixtieth birthday, I invited friends to an art gallery in my neighborhood. I had helped create three installations in an exhibit called, "Fruitful and Multiplying," curated by my friend, Minneapolis artist John Schuerman. He sought me out years before with a vision to invite artists to create art around the theme of overpopulation. I jumped at the chance. My installation was called, "The Goose the Deer and the Mirror." It was in the corner of the gallery and was exactly that: a taxidermied head of a deer, a full taxidermied Canada goose, and a mirror. John helped install it so visitors could see themselves in the mirror while they read this statement on the wall: "We can all exceed our carrying capacity." Another exhibit was just a metronome ticking at the same rate we are adding passengers to our limited planet. Never before had I participated in an artistic method of changing people's minds about an issue few dare to discuss.

We need more artists, writers, filmmakers, songwriters, choreographers, journalists, and critical thinkers to create new stories for our lives. The rich and powerful will fight us every step of the way, but the Earth hangs in the balance and must be fought for with all of the creative and critical thinking tools available to us.

Perhaps the salient point in this book is that we must see the world through multiple lenses. It may be efficient to work on one thing at a time or focus on one mission, but we must never assume it is the only narrative that will keep us afloat. No matter how passionate we are about an issue, we must make room for other narratives, for the world is a complex place.

I will end this journey with a poem I wrote as the Coronavirus became our loudest voice. It is my way of demonstrating one way we can bring out new stories in ways that people can hear them.

Under the Microscope
Ode to the Coronavirus

by Karen I Shragg

From under the microscope
You entered our discourse
Disrupting our lives
Inflaming our paranoia
Leaving pain and an eerie stillness in your wake
And grave diggers well employed
Yet in your ironic invisibility
Without scientific credentials
Without a Twitter account to call your own
You seem to be achieving the radical shift
Climate activists have been shrieking about
Overpopulation folks have been warning about
Scientists have been publishing about
You accomplished getting our collective attention
So fast it made our heads spin
And our portfolios flutter
Your voice has become the loudest one in the room
Silencing the banality none of us knew how to turn off
What activists have been trying to do for years with reasoned pleas,
Films, books and protests
You are achieving in just weeks of terror
We weren't able to knock the Ponzi scheme out of Wall Streets' sails
Or stop our love affair with crowded places
Factories from spewing
Or planes from flying
But you are halting our carbon loving ways
Stopping growth in its wildlife-killing tracks
In ways those not asleep at the wheel could only hope for
You leave us frightened and deeply saddened
That our humane tools of compassion, science and reason
were so weak
Compared to your grim reaper ways.

Epilogue

In 1789, James Madison crafted language defining the concepts of freedom of speech and freedom of the press, which evolved into a core rights in the First Amendment to the United States Constitution. Madison introduced the following to the United States House of Representatives, "The people shall not be deprived or abridged of their sentiments; and the freedom of the press, as one of the great bulwarks of liberty, shall be inviolable." His words revealed that 231 years ago, there was a new story brewing, one that countered what was happening to citizens back in the king's England.

Today in America we have multi-billionaires running agenda-based so-called news organizations. Newspapers are folding every day. Few independent news outlets can afford to keep their virtual doors open without allowing multi-national corporations to cover their budgets. To stay afloat, they have succumbed to the pressure to sell their soul, leaving Americans and other international viewers without the opportunity to hear the news through unfiltered voices. On top of it all, we want to stream entertainment and C-SPAN, with its direct footage of newsmakers 24/7, is just too dull for most consumers.

Madeline Weld, President of Population Institute Canada, said, "Without critical thought and freedom of the press a society becomes fossilized." To move the needle on any of these stories, our society needs to be free to discuss them in open public forums, in our work-places and in our legislatures. We have moved far away from those freedoms. The McCarthyism of the '50 s is alive and well, ready to cancel, fire or otherwise dismiss people who use everything from the wrong adjectives to the wrong pronouns in their speech. My cousin, a wonderful comedy writer for television in the '50s, was put on a list of suspected communists and not allowed to write professionally under his name for a while. Many lost their livelihoods and the world lost their innovative voices because intolerance took center stage.

There must be room for new ideas to take root. They cannot do so in an atmosphere riddled with suspicion and cancel culture. We need to find our way toward a more just world without going down this road again.

Joni Mitchells' words come to mind: "We are stardust, we are golden, we are billion-year-old carbon and we've got to get ourselves back to the garden." The garden of ideas and new stories will only flourish with the right amount of light (enlightenment), soil (scientific understanding), seeds (intentional desire for a better world), and permission to think and discuss freely beyond what we know.

Acknowledgements

Thank you to the publishers and editors at Freethought House press who have supported my writing for this my second book with them. In a world where free thinking, reading and publishing are becoming as uncommon as orangutans, I applaud your tenacity and fortitude and for keeping the lights on during extraordinarily tough times.

Thank you to my husband, John, for understanding that writing is a solitary 'sport' and that bouncing ideas off of him is a part of the game.

About the Author

Karen I. Shragg is a naturalist, author, poet, and overpopulation activist. She holds a doctorate in Critical Pedagogy, focused on social justice, from the University of St. Thomas, Minneapolis. Karen is the author of *Move Upstream: A Call to Solve Overpopulation*, which is used as a college textbook at both Roanoke College in Virginia and Tel Aviv University in Israel. She is also the author of three books of poetry, including *Organic Dreams and Pickled Nightmares*, and co-author of the *Nature's Yucky* children's series. Upon retiring from a 35-year career working at nature centers, Karen started Move Upstream Environmental Consulting, LLC, in January 2020 to continue her work on environmental projects. She is an active speaker on the topic of overpopulation, with speaking engagements throughout the United States, England and China. She serves on the advisory boards of World Population Balance and Earth Overshoot. Karen lives with her husband John in Bloomington, Minnesota. Her books, blog, and video interviews can be found at www.movingupstream.com.

www.ingramcontent.com/pod-product-compliance
Lightning Source LLC
Chambersburg PA
CBHW070914280326
41934CB00008B/1724